How to use this workbook

C000171137

Structure

The activities in this workbook will help you develop the skills and knowledge that you will need to achieve your best grade in A-level English Literature, whichever exam board specification you are following.

Each section offers a clear structure with activities that gradually increase in difficulty:

● **Starting out:** accessible activities that offer an introduction to the topic.
● **Developing your ideas:** skills-building activities that look in more detail at particular aspects of the text.
● **Taking it further:** more challenging tasks that will test your understanding of the text and consolidate your learning.

Boosting your skills

The final chapter of the workbook offers exam-focused activities that allow you to apply the skills you have developed. It also includes step-by-step guidance on the Assessment Objectives, and how to cover them in your written responses.

Features

Key terms

Definitions of key concepts and terminology. Understanding these and using them correctly in your written responses will help gain marks for AO1.

Key skills

Concise explanations of important skills to develop during your A-level studies. A variety of skills are covered, from fundamental ones such as analysing the structure of a text or embedding quotations in your writing, up to more advanced skills that are necessary to gain the top grades, such as exploring different interpretations of characters.

Challenge yourself

Advanced tasks that will push you further and help prepare you to achieve your best grade in the exams. They often focus on context (AO3), connections between texts (AO4) or critical interpretations of them (AO5).

Answers can be found at: **www.hoddereducation.co.uk/workbookanswers**

Introduction

King Lear is widely acknowledged as one of the greatest tragedies ever written. Shakespeare took the relatively straightforward, long-established story of King Leir – with its almost fairy-tale qualities of a king devising a love test for his three daughters – and transformed it into a bleak and almost unbearably moving study of evil, suffering and remorse.

As it charts Lear's tragic decline from a mighty, tyrannical king to a humble, foolish old man, the play asks its audiences to consider what defines power and authority, the nature of family bonds and the causes of suffering. Contextually, it is also an exploration of Jacobean ideas of kingship, gender and social hierarchy. Alongside this, in *King Lear* Shakespeare has written some of his most powerful poetry: the Romantic poet Percy Shelley judged it 'the most perfect specimen of dramatic poetry existing in the world'.

Studying *King Lear* at A-level and using this workbook

Your study of Shakespeare at GCSE will form a good basis as you approach *King Lear* for AS/A-level. However, you will now need to develop your existing skills alongside a more detailed understanding of the text. Activities in this workbook have been designed to support you in this process.

In particular, you will need to be more aware of different critical approaches, which is why this workbook devotes a chapter to them. Throughout the workbook, you will also encounter perspectives from a range of critics and other readers to help you to develop your own response to the play. You will also need to consider the historical, literary and social contexts of *King Lear*, and so a chapter in this workbook focuses in detail on how these aspects have influenced the play.

You will still need to study characterisation and themes at A-level, but you will be expected to have a deeper awareness of how these aspects function and are presented. The chapters 'Themes' and 'Characterisation' will refine your appreciation of Shakespeare's craft as a playwright as he dramatically presents his characters and develops his key ideas and concerns.

An important skill for students of literature is the ability to analyse the **ways** meanings are shaped. Activities in both the 'Language and imagery' and 'Plot and dramatic structure' chapters will draw further attention to how Shakespeare has crafted *King Lear*.

You need to develop your own interpretation of the play and be able to express this confidently, supporting your argument with evidence. The 'Key skills' boxes and the chapter 'Boosting your skills' will help you to write fluent, well-structured academic essays.

You do not necessarily have to attempt all the activities in the workbook: you could select according to your needs. However, there is a progression within each section, from the basics in 'Starting out' to the more challenging 'Taking it further' activities. In addition, 'Challenge yourself' boxes aim to help you achieve the top grades. You should also take note of the 'Key terms' boxes to widen your critical vocabulary.

Act, scene and line references are to the Arden edition, edited by R. A. Foakes.

Plot and dramatic structure

Not only will you need to have a secure understanding of the story of *King Lear*, you will also need to have a detailed awareness of how Shakespeare has **structured** the play: how and why he has put the play together in the way that he has. For example, you could consider the function of the Gloucester subplot and the way in which the play presents Lear's tragic decline.

Plot

STARTING OUT

1   Answer these questions to see how well you know the play.

(a) What is Cordelia's initial three-word response to Lear's 'love test'?

....

(b) Which two characters does Lear banish for displeasing him?

....

(c) What does Edmund do with the letter, supposedly from Edgar, when his father enters?

....

(d) Whom does Kent attack on his arrival at Gloucester's house?

....

(e) What does Kent read in the stocks?

....

(f) Name all the characters who meet on the heath.

....

(g) What smells of mortality?

....

(h) Who leads the blinded Gloucester supposedly to the cliff edge?

....

(i) Who wins the battle between France and Britain?

....

(j) When, according to Edgar, is Albany to sound the trumpet for a champion to appear?

....

(k) How does Goneril die?

....

(l) How does Regan die?

....

(m) Who carries the body of Cordelia on to the stage?

....

KEY SKILLS

Including textual details

Although you should avoid retelling the story, you should try to include textual details from the play to show you have a thorough understanding. For example, when quoting you could contextualise the reference: 'After learning that Gloucester has been in contact with Cordelia, Goneril suggests that they "pluck out his eyes".'

DEVELOPING YOUR IDEAS

2   In most of his plays Shakespeare adapts an existing story and *King Lear* is no exception. In fact, the story of King Lear (normally spelt King Leir) existed for over 400 years before Shakespeare's time and in many different variations. The oldest known version is in the Latin text *Historia Regum Britanniae*, written by Geoffrey of Monmouth (1136).

Read this summary of the Monmouth version of the story. Look for differences between it and the plot of Shakespeare's *King Lear*.

> As Leir is getting old, he plans to divide his kingdom and find husbands for his three daughters: Gonorilla, Regan and Cordeilla. He devises a love test in order to find out who should have the best husband and the best parts of his kingdom. Gonorilla passes the test and marries the Duke of Cornwall and Regan, also successful, marries the Duke of Albany. Cordeilla offends Leir in her answer. Against Leir's initial wishes, she marries the King of Gaul, but without her share of the kingdom. Cordeilla is sent to Gaul (France).
>
> Later, the Dukes of Albany and Cornwall rise against Leir and take his throne. His daughters then deprive him of his followers. Highly distressed, Leir flees to Gaul and is reunited with Cordeilla. The King of Gaul raises an army, successfully defeats the British forces and restores Leir to the throne.
>
> Three years later, Leir dies of old age. Cordeilla becomes Queen, but, after five years, she is overthrown by the sons of Gonorilla and Regan, who are incensed that Britain is being ruled by a woman. They imprison Cordeilla. Grieving for the loss of her kingdom, Cordeilla commits suicide.

In the table below, add what you think are the three most important changes (apart from names) and Shakespeare's possible reasons for making them.

CHANGE IN THE PLAY	POSSIBLE REASON(S)
1	
2	
3	

Challenge yourself

Many artists and writers have creatively revisited the story of *King Lear*. For example, Edward Bond's drama *Lear* is a political reimagining of Shakespeare's play. Jane Smiley's 1991 novel *A Thousand Acres* is a modern retelling, set on a large farm in Iowa, USA. Read either of these texts and consider what aspects of Shakespeare's original they have explored – and what aspects they have missed out.

TAKING IT FURTHER

3   The Russian author Leo Tolstoy famously wrote a withering attack on the play in his *Critical Essay on Shakespeare*. George Orwell, in another essay, remarked that Tolstoy found the plot of *King Lear* to be 'stupid', 'tedious' and 'full of incredible [unbelievable] events'. Do you agree? Explain your answer.

....

....

....

....

....

KEY SKILLS

Commenting on plot

You will earn little credit by simply retelling the story of the play. Examiners regard this as an indicator of a weak candidate. However, you could comment on how and why Shakespeare's plot differs from that of his main sources.

Dramatic structure

STARTING OUT

1   In which Act does each of these events occur?

EVENT		ACT
A	Cordelia sends her soldiers to search for Lear	
B	Gloucester is blinded	
C	Edmund persuades Gloucester that Edgar wishes his father was dead	
D	Edgar gives Albany the letter revealing Edmund and Goneril's plot against his life	
E	Kent argues with Oswald and challenges him to a fight	
F	Lear meets Poor Tom on the heath	
G	Lear and Cordelia are reunited and reconciled	
H	Edgar challenges Edmund and defeats him	

KEY SKILLS

Locating the passage

Some A-level English Literature exam questions require you to analyse a short passage from *King Lear*. You need to have a detailed understanding of plot and structure in order to locate the passage. You will need to identify where it appears in the plot and what happens of significance both before and after the passage.

DEVELOPING YOUR IDEAS

2 (a) *King Lear*'s structure is frequently described as complex, largely due to the relationships and parallels between the main plot and the highly developed subplot involving Gloucester, Edgar and Edmund.

Find quotations and details from both the main plot and the subplot for each of the headings in the table below.

MAIN PLOT (*KING LEAR*)		SUBPLOT (GLOUCESTER)
	A Deluded by deceitful children	
	B The good child is cast out	
	C Sibling rivalry	
	D Forced to live outside civilisation	
	E Extreme agony and suffering	
	F 'See' things more clearly	
	G Die of emotional shock	

CONTINUED

Answers can be found at: www.hoddereducation.co.uk/workbookanswers

(b) The two plots in *King Lear* are not entirely separate. List below three ways in which the two plotlines meet together. For example, Lear meets Edgar (outcast by his father, Gloucester, and disguised as Poor Tom) on the heath in Act 3.

(i) ....

....

(ii) ....

....

(iii) ....

....

(c) Look again at your completed table for Question 2(a). Why has Shakespeare included the Gloucester subplot? How does it contribute to themes and our understanding of Lear's situation?

....

....

....

....

....

3 (a) In many tragedies the tragic hero undergoes a reversal of fortune (known as peripeteia). In addition, the tragic hero may achieve some revelation or recognition of the errors he has made (which Aristotle called anagnorisis) and hence regain some status or nobility.

List **four** events in the play which you feel contribute towards Lear's tragic decline. Chart them on the graph provided.

Act 1   Act 2   Act 3   Act 4   Act 5

(b) Look again at your graph for Question 3(a). Which event do you think made the biggest single contribution to Lear's decline? Explain your answer.

....

....

....

CONTINUED ➡

(c) Where could you place Lear's anagnorisis on the graph? Explain your answer.

....

....

....

Peripeteia: The reversal of circumstances typically experienced by the tragic hero.

Anagnorisis: The moment in a tragedy in which the hero achieves some recognition or revelation of the errors of judgement he has made.

Challenge yourself

Shakespeare scholar A. C. Bradley criticised the Gloucester subplot in the play. He called it a 'structural weakness'. He argued that 'the number of essential characters is so large, their actions and movements are so complicated, and events towards the close crowd on one another so thickly, that the reader's attention, rapidly transferred from one centre of interest to another, is overstrained'. Do you agree with Bradley's assessment?

KEY SKILLS

Analysing structure

You need to demonstrate an understanding of how the structure of *King Lear* contributes to our understanding of the play as a whole, especially its ideas and themes.

TAKING IT FURTHER

4 This activity will test and consolidate your understanding of the play's plot and structure by asking you to locate and contextualise a passage. See if you can answer the questions **without** reading the rest of the scene.

Read the passage from Act 2 Scene 2 line 316 'Good morrow to you both' to line 353 'You taking airs with lameness!'

(a) Where has Lear been and where is he now?

....

(b) What has happened prior to this passage to make Lear turn against Goneril?

....

(c) How do Goneril and Regan treat and command Lear immediately **after** this passage?

....

....

(d) Crucially, where does Lear go at the end of Act 2 Scene 2 as a result of Regan's and Goneril's actions?

....

(e) How does this passage contribute to Lear's tragic decline (**peripeteia**)?

....

....

....

Themes

Themes are aspects of human experience and society that a literary text presents, explores and interrogates. Each reader or spectator may well identify or prioritise different themes in any given text – and this is especially the case for Shakespeare's plays. *King Lear* asks questions about what bonds us to our family and, perhaps most of all, about what it means to be human in an apparently cruel or uncaring world.

STARTING OUT

1   There is no definitive list of themes in *King Lear* – readers and spectators will discern or prioritise different concerns. Circle four themes from the list below that you think have central importance in *King Lear*.

Riches and poverty	Sight and blindness	Justice	Family
Madness	Science	Education	Kingship
The supernatural	Suffering	Disguise and clothing	Ambition

2   Look at the themes you have circled in the list above. Which do you think is the single most important theme in *King Lear*? Write a paragraph in which you explain your selection.

I think the most important theme in King Lear is ....

because ....

....

....

DEVELOPING YOUR IDEAS

3   Identify the speaker of each quotation and how the quotation relates to one or more of the themes listed below.

Sight and blindness   Family and loyalty   Madness   Nothingness

Suffering   Disguise and deception

A 'Nothing will come of nothing. Speak again.'

Speaker: .... Theme(s): ....

How it relates to theme(s): ....

....

B 'Still through the hawthorn blows the cold wind, says suum, mun, nonny, Dauphin my boy, my boy, *Cessez!* Let him trot by.'

Speaker: .... Theme(s): ....

How it relates to theme(s): ....

....

C 'I stumbled when I saw.'

Speaker: .... Theme(s): ....

How it relates to theme(s): ....

....

CONTINUED ➡

D 'As flies to wanton boys are we to the gods, / They kill us for their sport.'

Speaker: .... Theme(s): ....

How it relates to theme(s): ....

....

E 'How sharper than a serpent's tooth it is / To have a thankless child.'

Speaker: .... Theme(s): ....

How it relates to theme(s): ....

....

F 'My face I'll grime with filth, / Blanket my loins, elf all my hair in knots / And with presented nakedness outface / The winds'

Speaker: .... Theme(s): ....

How it relates to theme(s): ....

....

4   Look again at the quotations (A–F) for Question 3. Can you identify any distinctive features of language? Write the corresponding letter next to the appropriate language feature.

Simile: ....

Command: ....

Animal imagery: ....

Repetition: ....

> **Simile:** a figurative comparison, using the term 'like' or 'as'.

KEY SKILLS

Using terminology

Wherever it relates to your point, you should try to include specific and detailed literary terminology in your analysis.

Sight and blindness

5   There are 135 references in *King Lear* to sight, eyes, looking and blindness. In the space below, list quotations and references to sight and blindness you can remember from your reading of the play.

CONTINUED ➔

Answers can be found at: www.hoddereducation.co.uk/workbookanswers

6 KENT: See better, Lear, and let me still remain / The true blank of thine eye (1.1.159–60)

FOOL: So out went the candle and we were left darkling (1.4.208)

What are Kent and the Fool criticising Lear for?

....

....

....

7 Reread Act 3 Scene 7. Why does Shakespeare include the blinding of Gloucester in *King Lear*?

....

....

....

....

8 LEAR: No eyes in your head, nor no money in your purse? Your eyes are in a heavy case, your purse in a light, yet you see how this world goes.

GLOUCESTER: I see it feelingly.

LEAR: What, art mad? A man may see how this world goes with no eyes.
4.6.141–47

What have Gloucester and Lear come to 'see' about the world and their own actions? Refer to the above passage to help you in your answer.

....

....

....

....

....

Nature and family

The word 'nature' (including words like 'natural' and 'unnatural') occurs 51 times in *King Lear*. Nature, though, has several meanings in the play.

A It is used to refer to the 'natural' bond of family (and loyalty to the king), especially the love children bear towards their fathers (mothers are conspicuously absent in *King Lear*).

B Nature is distinguished from rigid social customs and conventions.

C Nature is part of the play's wider preoccupations with the 'nature of mankind' – what distinguishes us, if anything, from animals and monsters?

CONTINUED ➡

9   Read the quotations in the left hand column. Which of the above three aspects of nature in the play (A–C) most closely relate to the quotation? Go on to outline how the quotation develops ideas of nature in the play.

QUOTATION	A, B OR C?	HOW DOES THE QUOTATION DEVELOP IDEAS OF NATURE?
LEAR: [Cordelia is] a wretch whom nature is ashamed / Almost t'acknowledge hers. 1.1.212– 213	A	
LEAR: Unaccommodated man is no more but such a poor, bare, forked animal as thou art. 3.4.105– 106		
EDMUND: Thou, Nature, art my goddess; to thy law / My services are bound. Wherefore should I / Stand in the plague of custom? 1.2.1–3		
LEAR: Create her [Goneril] child of spleen, that it may live / And be a thwart disnatured torment to her. 1.4.274– 275		
LEAR: No, no, no life! / Why should a dog, a horse, a rat have life / And thou [Cordelia] no breath at all? 5.3.304–306		
KNIGHT: This night wherein the cub-drawn bear would couch, / The lion and the belly-pinched wolf / Keep their fur dry, unbonneted [Lear] runs, / And bids what will take all. 3.1.12–14		
LEAR: Allow not nature more than nature needs, / Man's life is as cheap as beast's. 2.2.455– 456		

Madness

10 Critics often claim that Lear's madness takes on different qualities as the play progresses. In Acts 1 and 2, Lear responds to situations and his daughters with wild (and disproportionate?) fury. In Acts 3 and 4, Lear, in his confused babblings, loses his capacity for reason and sense completely.

Find appropriate quotations from the play to support this view and complete the table on the following page.

CONTINUED

Answers can be found at: www.hoddereducation.co.uk/workbookanswers

ACTS 1 AND 2 – FURIOUS MADNESS	ACTS 3 AND 4 – CONFUSED BABBLINGS

11 How does the storm relate to Lear's madness?

....

....

....

....

12 What do you think is the impact of Poor Tom's madness? Look at the statements below in response to this question and circle the two you find most convincing.

A Poor Tom's madness provides much-needed comic relief in Act 3.

B It is painful to see Edgar's fake madness contrast with, and bring into a sharper focus, Lear's genuine madness.

C Poor Tom's wretched mental state allows Lear to empathise with the dispossessed.

D Poor Tom's behaviour, especially in Act 3, contributes to an overall sense of chaos and a meaningless universe, that the world is turned upside down.

E Poor Tom's mad ramblings and chants add to an unsettling feeling of menace and fear in the audience.

F Edgar's privilege as a nobleman, born into enormous wealth and power, is shown to be very vulnerable indeed through the presentation of Poor Tom's madness.

13 Critic Maynard Mack observed that Shakespearean tragic heroes – King Lear among them – frequently suffer madness as a form of punishment for their errors of judgement. However, this madness brings with it an 'insight' and 'the power to see the "truth"'.

Look at the passage below, from Act 3 Scene 4 lines 101–107. In it, a mad Lear is addressing a semi-naked Poor Tom (Edgar) in the storm. What 'insight' and 'truth' does Lear's madness bring?

Is man no more than this? Consider him well. Thou ow'st the worm no silk, the beast no hide, the sheep no wool, the cat no perfume. Ha? Here's three on's us [Kent, Lear and the Fool] are sophisticated; thou art the thing itself. Unaccommodated man is no more but such a poor, bare, forked animal as thou art. Off, off, you lendings: come, unbutton here. [*Tearing at his clothes, he is restrained by Kent and the Fool*]

CONTINUED ➤

....

....

....

....

....

Challenge yourself

How might this speech, in which a mad king wants to strip himself naked upon realising that the trappings of power and sophistication merely disguise a brutal humanity, have shocked a Jacobean audience?

Disguise and clothing

14 (a) What different disguises does Edgar adopt in the play?

....

....

....

(b) Find quotations or details from the play to support the view that the disguises of Caius (Kent) and Poor Tom (Edgar) are more valuable and useful than Kent and Edgar would otherwise be as merely banished aristocrats.

....

....

....

....

....

(c) How does Edmund deceive Edgar and Gloucester?

....

....

....

(d) How do Goneril and Regan (together and separately) deceive their father?

....

....

....

(e) Look at the following two quotations from the play which relate to clothing. Use them to write a paragraph on the play's presentation of the relationship between clothing and wealth and power.

Lear: Through tattered clothes great vices do appear; / Robes and furred gowns hide all. (4.6.160–1)

Lear: [to Regan] if only to go warm were gorgeous, / Why, nature needs not what thou gorgeous wear'st, / Which scarcely keeps thee warm. (2.2.457–9)

....

....

CONTINUED ➡

Answers can be found at: www.hoddereducation.co.uk/workbookanswers

....

....

....

....

....

....

Challenge yourself

In Act 3 Scene 4, after the 'unaccommodated man' speech (lines 99–107), the stage directions indicate that Lear tries to tear off his clothes. How far should a director allow Lear to get? Nothing more than a button or two? His shirt? All of his clothes? Famous naked Lears have included Ian Holm (National Theatre, 1997) and Ian McKellen (RSC, 2007–8). Do you think a naked Lear at this point would stand as a potent symbol of his absolute tragic decline?

Nothingness and suffering

15 Read the paragraph below on the idea of 'nothing' in the play. Fill the gaps using words from the list provided.

Cordelia's response to Lear's .... introduces a major concept in the play: nothing. The word 'nothing' or 'naught' occurs 34 times in the play. Regan and Goneril agree Lear can keep many of his .... of power, but, by Act 3, he is effectively left with nothing — no kingdom, no knights, no dignity, no .... and no clothes. And by the end of the play he even loses his last loving .... before he loses his own life. The play therefore explores what is left of our .... when everything that makes us who we are is .... The .... of King Lear is therefore a nihilistic one, full of .... and .... However, when they are reduced to nothing, Lear, Edgar and Gloucester all learn to .... the world more clearly and become............................... . So the audience is perhaps left to ponder: does .... really come of nothing?

trappings	anarchy	nothing	see	hope	stripped away
wiser	embellished	hate	love test	suffering	something
friend	sanity	daughter	humanity	world	

16 Critic David Kastan argues that in Shakespeare's tragedies, like *King Lear*, suffering is not only absolutely central, but Shakespeare offers no *explanation* of the suffering. When Lear, holding his dead child, cries 'Why should a dog, a horse, a rat have life / And thou no breath at all?' no answer is forthcoming. 'Directly questioning [the] world', Kastan writes, 'produces no more satisfying responses ... these are the unanswered (perhaps unanswerable) questions of the tragic world ... for Shakespeare, anyhow, the uncertainty is the point.'

CONTINUED

Write a paragraph responding to Kastan's view. Consider:
- How does Lear suffer?
- Why does he suffer?
- Does the play provide any comfort or explanation, religious or otherwise?

....

....

....

....

....

....

....

Challenge yourself

Kastan's views in Question 16 do not just apply to *King Lear* – indeed, he claimed that they apply to all of Shakespeare's tragedies. Read Shakespeare's *Hamlet* or watch a film version. What kind of questions does this play ask? Are any answers provided? How does Hamlet suffer?

KEY SKILLS

Do themes connect?

Although you should always ensure you answer the question, do not see each theme as completely separate from the others. Different themes often intersect, contradict or are explored in the same quotation or passage. For example, through his exploration of **sight and blindness**, we could argue that Shakespeare is actually saying something equally significant about the **nature** of mankind.

TAKING IT FURTHER

17 This section of the workbook has guided you through the following themes in *King Lear*:

> Sight and blindness
>
> Nature and family
>
> Madness
>
> Disguise and clothing
>
> Nothingness and suffering

Choose one of these themes (perhaps the one you are **least** confident about) and write it in the gap on the following exam-style essay question:

Examine the presentation of .... **in** *King Lear*.

Using some of your answers to the activities in this section to help you, write a detailed essay plan for your chosen question. Use a separate piece of paper.

Characterisation

To get to grips with the characters in *King Lear*, you need to think about how they are used by Shakespeare not only to develop the plot but also to explore or represent themes and ideas. You need to show an appreciation of Shakespeare's **craft** in conveying and developing characters, such as through the way they use language, the way they interact with other characters, any suggested stage directions, and also any soliloquies and asides. You might also need to evaluate different interpretations and consider the impact of contexts.

Character overview

STARTING OUT

1 Identify which character is referred to in each description below. NOTE: A character may match more than one description.

DESCRIPTION	CHARACTER
A A Machiavellian villain	
B Lear's oldest daughter	
C Was played originally by Robert Armin, who played Feste in *Twelfth Night*	
D She poisons her sister	
E She stabs a servant	
F Believes in astrological forecasts	
G Adopts many disguises throughout the play	
H Adopts the role of Caius	
I He blinds Gloucester	
J Is killed by Edgar in Act 4	

2 (a) Characters in *King Lear* can be paired off with one another. Match the characters in the right-hand column with characters in the left.

Lear
Kent
Albany
Cordelia
France
Edgar

Burgundy
Goneril
Edmund
Oswald
Cornwall
Gloucester

(b) Pick a single 'pairing' from Question 2(a) and write a summary of the similarities and differences between the two characters.

....

....

....

....

....

....

CONTINUED ➡

3 Draw a line to match the quotation with the character.

QUOTATION		CHARACTER
A	We have seen the best of our time.	Regan
B	Look there, look there!	Goneril
C	Now, by my life / Old fools are babes again and must be used / With checks as flatteries, when they are seen abused.	Gloucester
D	This cold night will turn us all to fools and madmen.	Cordelia
E	O you kind gods! / Cure this great breach in his abused nature; / Th'untuned and jarring senses, O, wind up / Of this child-changed father.	Fool
F	Go, thrust him out at gates and let him smell / His way to Dover	Lear
G	Vex not his ghost; O, let him pass.	Kent

DEVELOPING YOUR IDEAS

4 Choose one of the quotations from Question 3 and explain how it develops the character.

....

....

TAKING IT FURTHER

5 On a separate piece of paper, write at least two paragraphs giving your views on this statement:

'All the major characters in *King Lear* confirm that the play takes an incredibly pessimistic view of human nature.'

KEY SKILLS

Characters are fictional constructs

Avoid writing about characters as though they were real people. Demonstrate to the examiner that you are aware that they are fictional constructs by using expressions like 'Lear is shown to be …'; 'Regan is presented as …'; 'Edmund is constructed as …'.

Lear

STARTING OUT

1 Circle the words below that you think most apply to Lear:

tyrant   victim   weak   angry   loving father   foolish   humble

DEVELOPING YOUR IDEAS

2 Describe in your own words how Lear's initial decisions to divide his kingdom, remain king and conduct the love test with his daughters are **errors of judgement**.

....

....

....

CONTINUED ➡

Answers can be found at: www.hoddereducation.co.uk/workbookanswers

3 Read this speech from Lear to Goneril (from Act 1 Scene 4) and annotate it to show what key character traits the highlighted lines indicate in Lear:

> I am <u>ashamed</u>
> <u>That thou hast power to shake my manhood</u>[1] thus;
> That these hot tears, which break from me perforce,
> Should make thee worth them. <u>Blasts and fogs upon thee!</u>[2]
> Th'untented woundings of a father's curse
> Pierce every sense about thee. <u>Old fond eyes,</u>
> <u>Beweep this cause again, I'll pluck ye out</u>[3],
> And cast you, with the waters that you loose
> To temper clay. Yea, is't come to this?
> Ha? Let it be so. Yet have <u>I left a daughter,</u>
> <u>Who I am sure is kind and comfortable</u>[4].
> When she shall hear this of thee with her nails
> She'll flay thy wolvish visage. <u>Thou shalt find</u>
> <u>That I'll resume the shape which thou dost think</u>
> <u>I have cast off for ever</u>[5]. Thou shalt, I warrant thee.

4 Do you feel this speech develops sympathy for Lear?

....

....

5 In his classic analysis *Poetics*, Greek philosopher Aristotle (384–322 BCE) identified some of the following features of the tragic heroes and heroines in classical tragedies. Apply these features to Lear in *King Lear* by completing the table.

FEATURE OF A TRAGIC HERO / HEROINE	EVIDENCE
A One of the main aims of a tragedy is to make the audience feel pity (**pathos**) for the hero.	
B Another important aim of a tragedy is to make the audience feel terror and fear for the fate of the hero.	

CONTINUED ➔

FEATURE OF A TRAGIC HERO / HEROINE	EVIDENCE
C The tragic hero is identifiably 'human' – that is, neither entirely good nor entirely bad – so we can identify with his or her plight.	
D The tragic hero is normally of noble birth and has a higher social status.	
E A tragedy describes the hero's fall from status and prosperity to desolation, isolation and, often, madness. This reversal of fortune can be called **peripeteia**.	
F The tragic decline is brought about in part by a tragic flaw or error of judgement in the hero, known as his **hamartia**.	
G The tragic hero experiences **anagnorisis** – a moment of recognition or discovery, often of his or her own mistakes and errors of judgement. Usually, this moment of clarity comes too late for the hero to effect any change.	
H The tragic hero dies at the end of the tragedy.	

Challenge yourself

Many commentators have identified a similarity between the character of Lear and the figure of Job, from the Old Testament of the Bible. Job is a good man who seemingly suffers at the hands of God. Conduct some research into Job, or read the Book of Job in the Bible, and chart similarities and differences between these two characters.

6   Many commentators observe substantial changes in Lear's character. His behaviour and values change remarkably throughout the play. He begins the play as king and tyrant; he undergoes suffering and madness and emerges at the end a wiser, humble old man.

Number these quotations from the play in order from 1 to 10. Add a note on how each quotation shows the changing character of Lear. Start by working out the first and last lines.

	QUOTATION	ORDER 1–10	HOW IT SUGGESTS CHANGES IN LEAR'S CHARACTER
A	If ... thy banished trunk be found in our dominions, / The moment is thy death. Away! By Jupiter, / This shall not be revoked.	3	
B	Blow winds and crack your cheeks! Rage, blow! / You cataracts and hurricanoes, spout / Till you have drenched our steeples	4	
C	Tell me, my daughters ... Which of you shall we say doth love us most, / That we our largest bounty may extend.		
D	My wits begin to turn.		
E	I might have saved her; now she's gone for ever. / Cordelia, Cordelia, stay a little.		
F	I am a very foolish, fond old man.		
G	Here I disclaim all my paternal care, / Propinquity and property of blood, / And as a stranger to my heart and me / Hold thee from this for ever.		

CONTINUED ➡

QUOTATION	ORDER 1–10	HOW IT SUGGESTS CHANGES IN LEAR'S CHARACTER
H	How shall your houseless heads and unfed sides, / Your looped and windowed raggedness, defend you / From seasons such as these? O, I have ta'en / Too little care of this.		
I	And the creature run from the cur – there thou mightst behold the great image of authority: a dog's obeyed in office.		
J	I'll kneel down / And ask of thee forgiveness.		

7 Referring to Question 6, summarise how Lear changes during the course of the play and show how this relates to the genre of tragedy as shown in Question 5.

....

....

....

....

....

....

....

TAKING IT FURTHER

8 Which of the following two views on the character of Lear do you agree with more and why? Write your answer on the following page.

A King Lear is a vain, tyrannical and demanding father and king who has brought about his own downfall and the death of Cordelia.

B It is reasonable for an 80-year-old man to long for retirement. Lear could not have expected his daughters' ungrateful cruelty and ambition. He is a suffering victim who inspires admiration and affection.

CONTINUED

....

....

....

....

....

....

....

KEY SKILLS

Supporting your argument

You should always support your argument – even if it is based on a critical perspective – through detailed references to the play.

Cordelia

STARTING OUT

1   Read the quotations below and circle those which are describing or addressed to Cordelia. Go on to identify the speaker of each quotation as well.

(a) I loved her most, and thought to set my rest / On her kind nursery

(b) [You] are most rich being poor ... Thee and thy virtues here I seize upon

(c) Detested kite, thou liest.

(d) The barbarous Scythian, ... shall to my bosom / Be as well neighboured, pitied and relieved, / As thou.

(e) Thou shalt never have my curse. / Thy tender-hafted nature shall not give / Thee o'er to harshness.

(f) She shook / The holy water from her heavenly eyes.

DEVELOPING YOUR IDEAS

2   A. C. Bradley says that Cordelia appears in 'only four of the twenty-six scenes' and she speaks 'scarcely more than a hundred lines'. However, Bradley, like many commentators, identifies her as having a 'wonderful' central role, embodying saintly Christian values (despite the play's ostensibly pagan setting) such as forgiveness, honesty and purity.

Skim through the play, especially the scenes in which she appears (1.1, 4.4, 4.7, 5.3 – and she is described in 4.3), and find six religious words and phrases associated with her, such as 'The holy water from her heavenly eyes'.

1	
2	
3	
4	
5	
6	

3   Read the passage from Act 4 Scene 7, beginning with line 26 'O my dear father' and ending line 75 'No cause, no cause' and answer the following questions.

(a) What implied stage direction can you discern in line 27? What does Cordelia hope this action will bring?

....

(b) How is Cordelia's pity for her father suggested in her longer speech beginning on line 30?

....

....

....

....

(c) Given the context of this passage within the rest of the play, what is the significance of Cordelia calling her father 'my royal lord' on line 44?

....

....

(d) Which of Lear's utterances confirm Cordelia as a saintly being?

....

CONTINUED ➡

Answers can be found at: www.hoddereducation.co.uk/workbookanswers

(e) Comment on the significance of the 'kneeling' in the stage directions.

....

....

....

(f) What does Cordelia mean by the repeated phrase 'No cause, no cause'? What does this suggest about her character?

....

....

....

KEY SKILLS

Focusing on a passage

Even if the exam question asks you to look at the play as a whole, it can be useful to spend some time in your response focusing on a particular passage (as you did for Question 3). This will help you to demonstrate a detailed appreciation of Shakespeare's crafting of the play, as well as a specific awareness of how relationships, characters and ideas develop within the passage.

TAKING IT FURTHER

4   Certainly, Cordelia's most significant action in the play is her honest answer to Lear's love test. How do you respond to Cordelia's answer? Two views are outlined below. Choose the view you agree with the most and, beneath, briefly explain why you agree. Beneath the other view, explain why you disagree (or agree less).

Cordelia is to be blamed for the disastrous consequences of her conduct in Act 1 Scene 1. Her refusal is especially problematic, as she clearly knows how evil her sisters are. Her love for her father is undisputed, so why does she put her honesty first above all else?

....

....

....

Cordelia is a consistently virtuous character, held in high esteem by 'good' characters such as Kent. Her refusal to participate in the contest is a sign of her integrity as well as an attempt to alert Lear to his poor judgement.

....

....

....

Goneril and Regan

STARTING OUT

1 (a) Goneril and Regan share many characteristics: cold, ambitious, predatory. They both destroy the 'natural' bond of family and the state and are agents of chaos set against a cruel and uncaring world. However, you will need to have an awareness of the differences between Goneril and Regan as well.

Circle the statements which describe Goneril; underline the statements which describe Regan.

Kills a servant

The oldest sister

Takes an initial lead role in planning how to respond to their father's behaviour

Provokes the first confrontation with her father

Suggests or urges the gouging of Gloucester's second eye

Suggests they lock the doors on Lear to teach him a lesson

Poisons her sister

Urges further punishment of Kent

(b) Summarise the main differences between Goneril and Regan.

....

....

....

....

DEVELOPING YOUR IDEAS

2 (a) Feminist critics have observed that Goneril and Regan are presented as monstrous and unnatural – by both the play and Lear himself – because they adopt qualities associated with masculinity. In the table below, list three things either Goneril and/or Regan do or say which might typically be associated with masculinity.

1	
2	
3	

(b) How might a Jacobean audience's response to Goneril and Regan differ from that of a modern audience?

....

....

....

....

TAKING IT FURTHER

3   Kathleen McLuskie in her essay 'The Patriarchal Bard: Feminist Criticism and King Lear' argues that Goneril and Regan's gender 'insubordination' is shown to result in chaos because it threatens male power. She argues that, since the play is patriarchal, Goneril and Regan must be shown to be monstrous and unnatural, and they must be punished.

Look at your response to Question 2. Do any of these support the views expressed by McLuskie? Does this perspective change the way you respond to Goneril and Regan?

....

....

....

....

....

....

Patriarchy, patriarchal: A society in which men are in positions of power and influence. It is a key concept in feminist literary criticism.

Gloucester

STARTING OUT

1   Find a quotation to support each of these aspects of Gloucester's character:

Brave and courageous	
Suicidal	
Adulterous	
Trusting / easily manipulated	
Loyal (to Lear)	

DEVELOPING YOUR IDEAS

2   Look again at your quotation for 'suicidal' in Question 1 and write it up into an analytical paragraph. Think especially about the impact suicidal contemplations might have on the wider concerns of the play.

....

....

....

....

....

CONTINUED ➡

3   Look again at your quotation for 'Brave and courageous' and write it up into an analytical paragraph. Think especially about why Shakespeare wanted to give Gloucester these admirable qualities.

....

....

....

....

....

....

....

KEY SKILLS

Stage action and implied stage directions

Remember that characters do not exist solely on the page. They are to be interpreted by actors and performed live on stage. One way you can demonstrate an awareness of this is to consider, where appropriate, the impact of stage action (such as the dramatic combat between Edgar and Edmund) and implied stage directions (for example, when Lear says 'Be your tears wet?' to Cordelia, Shakespeare is implying that Cordelia is crying at this point).

TAKING IT FURTHER

4   Gloucester has two important roles in the play. He is a **foil** for Lear and parallels him in many ways: they both have a moral crisis over their children, bring disaster by trusting the wrong child(ren) and move to understanding and forgiveness. Another role Gloucester has is to further the play's exploration of **suffering**.

   (a) List five different ways in which Gloucester suffers in the play.

   - ....
   - ....
   - ....
   - ....
   - ....

   (b) 'Men must endure / Their going hence even as their coming hither. / Ripeness is all'. **How does Edgar advise Gloucester to respond to suffering?**

   ....

   ....

   ....

   (c) Using your answers to the preceding activities on Gloucester, write two paragraphs on a separate piece of paper in response to this essay question:

   'As flies to wanton boys, are we to th' gods, / They kill us for their sport.' To what extent can this pessimistic judgement be applied to the presentation of Gloucester in King Lear?

Foil: A character who clearly contrasts with another character in order to draw the audience's attention towards particular qualities or aspects of the other character.

Edmund

STARTING OUT

1   What does soliloquy mean? How might a soliloquy affect the audience's relationship with the character delivering the soliloquy?

   ....

   ....

2   List the different ways in which Edmund deceives other characters in *King Lear*.

   ●   ....

   ●   ....

   ●   ....

   ●   ....

   ●   ....

   ●   ....

3   Summarise how Edmund's actions lead directly to the death of:

   (a) Goneril

   ....

   ....

   (b) Regan

   ....

   ....

   (c) Cordelia

   ....

   ....

   (d) Lear

   ....

   ....

DEVELOPING YOUR IDEAS

4   Annotate the soliloquy below with answers to the following questions:

(a) Edmund is here addressing and invoking Nature as a personified goddess and agreeing to bind himself to her laws. What 'laws' might they be? How is nature being depicted here?

(b) What does 'plague of custom' mean? What is Edmund rebelling against?

(c) Comment on Shakespeare's use of repetition here.

(d) How is Edmund depicting lovemaking in marriage? How does this contrast with Gloucester's use of the word 'sport' in 1.1?

(e) What does the repeated structure of 'I grow, I prosper' imply about Edmund's mood?

(f) How might a Jacobean audience have found this final, concluding command particularly shocking?

> Thou, Nature, art my goddess[a]; to thy law
>
> My services are bound. Wherefore should I
>
> Stand in the plague of custom[b], and permit
>
> The curiosity of nations to deprive me?
>
> For that I am some twelve or fourteen moon-shines
>
> Lag of a brother? Why bastard? Wherefore base?
>
> When my dimensions are as well compact,
>
> My mind as generous, and my shape as true,
>
> As honest madam's issue? Why brand they us
>
> With base? With baseness, bastardy? Base, base?[c]
>
> Who, in the lusty stealth of nature, take
>
> More composition and fierce quality
>
> Than doth, within a dull stale tired bed[d]
>
> Go to the creating of a whole tribe of fops
>
> Got 'tween asleep and wake. Well, then,
>
> Legitimate Edgar, I must have your land.
>
> Our father's love is to the bastard Edmund
>
> As to the legitimate. Fine word, 'legitimate'!
>
> Well, my legitimate, if this letter speed
>
> And my invention thrive, Edmund the base
>
> Shall top the legitimate. I grow, I prosper[e]:
>
> Now, gods, stand up for bastards[f]!

Challenge yourself

Edmund is presented as a Machiavellian villain. Based on the political writings of Niccolò Machiavelli, Renaissance playwrights often included a Machiavellian villain in their tragedies. These characters are typified by scheming and ruthless ambition. Conduct some further research into Machiavellian villains and read or watch *Richard III*, perhaps Shakespeare's most famous example of this type of character.

TAKING IT FURTHER

5 Using Question 4 as a model, annotate this section of Edmund's soliloquy in Act 5 Scene 1 (lines 56–70). Edmund is here reflecting on the natures of Goneril and Regan, to both of whom he has sworn his love.

> To both these sisters have I sworn my love,
>
> Each jealous of the other, as the stung
>
> Are of the adder. Which of them shall I take?
>
> Both? One? Or neither? Neither can be enjoyed,
>
> If both remain alive. To take the widow
>
> Exasperates, makes mad her sister Goneril,
>
> And hardly shall I carry out my side,
>
> Her husband being alive. Now then, we'll use
>
> His countenance for the battle, which being done,
>
> Let her who would be rid of him devise
>
> His speedy taking off. As for the mercy
>
> Which he intends to Lear and to Cordelia,
>
> The battle done, and they within our power,
>
> Shall never see his pardon; for my state
>
> Stands on me to defend, not to debate.

Challenge yourself

Is Edmund really a radical rebel against Jacobean society? Does he not just want to succeed on society's terms by being accepted as an aristocratic heir and duke? Is he really such an anti-establishment figure?

Edgar

STARTING OUT

1 Summarise the important differences between the half-brothers Edgar and Edmund.

....

....

....

....

DEVELOPING YOUR IDEAS

2   Many commentators identify significant changes – even a progression – in Edgar's characterisation. He grows in heroic stature as the plot develops. The literary scholar Kenneth Muir argues that 'The various roles he plays are the means by which he matures into royalty.'

Match the quotations below with one of the six aspects of Edgar's character.

1	2	3	4	5	6
Innocent and gullible	A poor, mad beggar	A moral redeemer of his father	A protector of his father's life	An agent of justice	A (wise) king of Britain

	QUOTATION	ASPECT OF CHARACTER (1–6)
A	Why I do trifle thus with his despair / Is done to cure it.	3
B	A most toad-spotted traitor... / This sword, this arm and my best spirits are bent / To prove upon thy heart ... / Thou [Edmund] liest.	
C	Whose nature is so far from doing harms / That he suspects none (Edmund on Edgar)	
D	Friends of my soul, you twain, / Rule in this realm and the gored state sustain.	
E	To take the basest and most poorest shape / That ever penury in contempt of man / Brought near to beast.	
F	I'se try whether your costard [head] or my baton be the harder. Ch'ill be plain with you. (Edgar talking to Oswald)	

TAKING IT FURTHER

3   Other commentators, however, do not see such progress and 'depth' to Edgar's characterisation. Some see him as merely a lacklustre plot device, especially against the titanic Lear. Edgar's 'various roles do not tell us more about Edgar. They tell us more about the play in which he is a character' (Leo Kirschbaum). On a separate piece of paper, write a paragraph, including at least two references to the play, in which you argue in favour of Kirschbaum's view.

KEY SKILLS

Different interpretations of character

In your essays, you may need to show how different interpretations have influenced your ideas about Shakespeare's characterisation. Consider using the paragraph you wrote for Question 3 as one model for demonstrating this skill to the examiner.

The Fool

STARTING OUT

1   One of the Fool's main functions in the play is to push Lear towards seeing the truth. Find three quotations from *King Lear* where you feel the Fool is fulfilling this function.

1	
2	
3	

DEVELOPING YOUR IDEAS

2   Read the paragraph below on the Fool. Fill the gaps using words from the list provided.

The Fool is perhaps the most remarkable creation in King Lear and he has long puzzled audiences and critics. There is, of course, a 'clown' part in all the great tragedies, such as the Gravedigger in .... and the Drunken Porter in .... , but the Fool in King Lear is a fully .... character in the drama.

Following the departure of Will Kemp in around 1600, ... was the leading comedy actor in Shakespeare's group of actors and would have played the Fool in the first performances of King Lear.

The licensed fool or 'Court Jesters' were associated with .... Kings in Shakespeare's time, but Henry VIII did have a court jester called .... , who called his king ....

The Fool has many roles in the play: he .... the powerful and the wealthy, he is a substitute for .... , he develops pathos as he suffers alongside Lear and he provides some much-needed comic .... from the play's tragic desolation. Primarily, though, his role seems to be to tell the .... to Lear about his errors of judgement: 'thou mad'st thy daughters thy ....' , he says, and 'all thy other titles thou hast given away; that thou wast born with'.

Why does the Fool disappear after Act 3 Scene 6? Perhaps Shakespeare felt his presence would be out of place amidst the .... of the play's final scenes.

Cordelia	uncle	*Romeo and Juliet*	integrated	Richard Armin	medieval
your majesty	satirises	Goneril	relief	truth	mothers
Macbeth	victims	*Hamlet*	happiness	Will Somers	devastation
supports					

TAKING IT FURTHER

3   The poet John Keats wrote 'Does not the Fool by his very levity give a finishing touch to the pathos [pity]; making what without him would be within our heart-reach, nearly unfathomable?'
Reread Act 1 Scene 4 lines 93–314 and, in the light of Keats's comments, write an essay plan on the role of the Fool in this scene. Use a separate piece of paper.

Writer's methods: Language and imagery

An important skill for students of literature is the ability to analyse the **ways** in which meanings are shaped. These activities will draw your attention to Shakespeare's use of language and imagery in particular. Shakespeare uses different clusters of images, such as animals and clothing. You will also consider the significance of prose and blank verse.

STARTING OUT

1   Match each line below to the literary technique and comment briefly on the effects. Techniques may occur more than once. Choose from:

epizeuxis	rhetorical question	simile	invocation
imperative	hyperbole	metaphor	string of adjectives

(a) GLOUCESTER: As flies to wanton boys are we to the gods, / They kill us for their sport.

....

....

(b) CORDELIA: No cause, no cause.

....

....

(c) GONERIL: I do love you more than word can wield the matter/ Dearer than eyesight, space and liberty, / Beyond what can be valued, rich or rare

....

....

(d) LEAR: You are men of stones!

....

....

(e) LEAR: Here I stand ... A poor, infirm, weak and despised old man.

....

....

(f) LEAR: Never, never, never, never, never.

....

....

(g) EDMUND: Wherefore should I / Stand in the plague of custom, and permit / The curiosity of nations to deprive me?

....

....

(h) GONERIL: Get you gone, / And hasten your return.

....

....

CONTINUED ➡

(i) LEAR: The bow is bent and drawn; make from the shaft.

....

....

(j) LEAR: Hear, Nature, hear, dear goddess.

....

....

> **Epizeuxis:** The repetition of a word or phrase in immediate succession.
> **Rhetorical question:** A question asked to make a point or for effect rather than to get an answer.
> **Invocation:** An address to a god or a higher being, normally requesting support or assistance in some way.
> **Imperative:** A command. Imperatives usually begin with a main verb, such as '**Close** the window'.
> **Hyperbole:** Deliberate exaggeration for rhetorical effect.
> **String of adjectives:** A list of adjectives all describing the same noun.

KEY SKILLS

Integrating literary terminology

Weave your identification of a technique into a sentence in which you analyse its effects. For example: 'The imperatives by which Goneril commands Oswald to exit and 'hasten' his return confirm Goneril as a very powerful woman who exerts absolute control over events and other characters.'

2   Read the Key Skills box above. Write a similar sentence evaluating the effects of three of the remaining quotations for Question 1.

(a) ....

....

(b) ....

....

(c) ....

....

DEVELOPING YOUR IDEAS

Imagery

3   Divide the following images into different categories according to their content. For example, some are images of clothing.

| A   Disease that's in my flesh | B   Off, off, you lendings | C   Wolfish visage |

| D   The true blank of thine eye | E   Pelican daughters |

| F   Three suits to his back, six shirts to his body | G   Your eyes are in a heavy case |

| H   All the plagues that in the pendulous air hang | I   A boil, / A plague sore, or embossed carbuncle |

| J   Furred gowns hide all | K   Upon these eyes of thine I'll set my foot | L   Detested kite |

CONTINUED ➡

GROUP 1	Clothing	EXAMPLES	
GROUP 2		EXAMPLES	
GROUP 3		EXAMPLES	
GROUP 4		EXAMPLES	

4   The preceding activity drew your attention towards some of the images and references that recur throughout the play. These images relate very closely to the play's network of themes (a quick glance at your completed table above should confirm this).

Many readers identify **animal imagery** as particularly prominent. Critic Martin Old claims there are '143 direct references to 67 different animals and approximately 15 indirect references to beasts, creatures or monsters' in *King Lear*.

(a) There are 34 mentions of dogs. Find three and write them below.

   (i) ....

   (ii) ....

   (iii) ....

(b) There are 14 references to different types of birds. Find two and write them below.

   (i) ....

   (ii) ....

(c) There are eight references to monsters. Find two and write them below.

   (i) ....

   (ii) ....

(d) There are six references to wolves, six references to bears and five to foxes. Find any two of these and write them below.

   (i) ....

   (ii) ....

5   Why does Shakespeare include so many references to – and images of – animals in *King Lear*? You may write more than one reason.

   ....

   ....

   ....

   ....

   ....

   ....

CONTINUED ➡

6   Circle the best words from the options below to complete the two paragraphs on the play's images of **disease and pain**.

The political and moral [disruptions / nourishments / regeneration / comedy] which result from Lear's division of his kingdom find parallels in recurring [similes / images / verbs / imperatives] of disease and pain. Indeed, critic Caroline Spurgeon finds 'only one overpowering and dominating image' in *King Lear*: that of a body racked and tortured. She argues that the play persistently provides [beautiful / metaphorical / literal / approximate] reminders of a human body in anguished movement, such as 'tugged', 'flayed', 'scalded' and 'broken'. Disease and pain are appropriate to the wider concerns of a play which interrogates the base nature of humanity, of what we become when civilisation gets stripped away. These images contribute to the overall [consoling / redeeming / terrifying / reflective] dramatic effect of the play.

For a specific example, Lear calls Goneril 'a boil, / A plague sore, or embossed carbuncle / In my corrupted blood'. This vivid tripling of [adjectives / metaphors / similes / puns] angrily depicts Goneril as a horrific disease and further associates her with [Regan / joy / monstrosity / femininity], especially to a Jacobean audience who would have experienced terrifying and frequent outbreaks of the bubonic plague.

The language of religion

7   The question of whether or not *King Lear* is a Christian play is open to debate. The setting is pagan, and there are some references to pre-Christian gods. But the play contains many Christian references and associations as well: characters learn through Christ-like suffering and Cordelia is presented as a saintly character.

(a) When is *King Lear* set?

....

(b) Shakespeare included (often anachronistic) references to pagan, pre-Christian gods. Find two.

- ....

....

- ....

....

(c) A number of characters in the play utter prayers and invocations to these pagan gods. Find two. Write down the act, scene and line numbers and summarise for each what you think the character is asking of the gods.

- ....

....

- ....

....

(d) Edgar, in Act 5 Scene 3, says 'The gods are just and of our pleasant vices / Make instruments to plague us.' Do you think the play presents the gods as being 'just'? Or are they just playing a grim game with the characters, like 'wanton boys' with 'flies'? Support your answer with references to the play.

....

....

....

....

(e) Some find *King Lear* to be a Christian play. Read Act 4 Scene 3 and find words and phrases which confirm this view.

....

....

....

CONTINUED ➔

Challenge yourself

Early twentieth-century critics identified *King Lear* as a Christian play. A.C. Bradley wrote that virtue and goodness ultimately triumph in spite of the suffering. Critic G. Wilson Knight also, despite acknowledging the grotesque absurdity of the play, ultimately saw in it a very Christian notion of redemption: Cordelia's love is Christ-like and Lear is redeemed through suffering. Do you find these interpretations convincing?

The changing language of King Lear

8   Lear's language changes in the course of the play.

   (a) Annotate in the passage below examples of the following characteristics of Lear's use of language at the **beginning** of the play:

   - direct and confident commands (imperatives)
   - the royal 'we'
   - interruptions
   - the ways in which Lear is addressed by other characters
   - associations with anger
   - listing
   - other words associated with kingly authority.

   KENT   Good my liege,–

   LEAR Peace, Kent!

   Come not between the dragon and his wrath!

   I loved her most, and thought to set my rest

   On her kind nursery. [*to Cordelia*] Hence, and avoid my sight.

   So be my grave my peace, as here I give

   Her father's heart from her. Call France. Who stirs?

   Call Burgundy. Cornwall and Albany,

   With my two daughters' dowers digest this third.

   Let pride, which she calls plainness, marry her.

   I do invest you jointly with my power,

   Pre-eminence, and all the large effects

   That troop with majesty. Ourself by monthly course,

   With reservation of an hundred knights

   By you to be sustained, shall our abode

   Make with you by due turn; only we still retain

   The name, and all th'addition to a king: the sway,

   Revenue, execution of the rest,

   Beloved sons, be yours; which to confirm,

   This coronet part betwixt you.

CONTINUED

Answers can be found at: www.hoddereducation.co.uk/workbookanswers

> **KENT**   Royal Lear,
>
> Whom I have ever honoured as my king,
>
> Loved as my father, as my master followed,
>
> As my great patron thought on in my prayers–
>
> **LEAR** The bow is bent and drawn, make from the shaft.

(b) Find and annotate in the passage below examples of some of the following characteristics of Lear's use of language at the **end** of the play:
   - words associated with Christianity and humility
   - imagery, especially similes
   - pronoun use
   - listing
   - commands (imperatives)
   - other noteworthy differences with the previous passage.

> **LEAR**   Come, let's away to prison;
>
> We two alone will sing like birds I' the cage.
>
> When thou dost ask me blessing I'll kneel down
>
> And ask of thee forgiveness. So we'll live
>
> And pray, and sing, and tell old tales, and laugh
>
> At gilded butterflies, and hear poor rogues
>
> Talk of court news; and we'll talk with them too –
>
> Who loses and who wins, who's in, who's out –
>
> And take upon's the mystery of things
>
> As if we were God's spies. And we'll wear out
>
> In a walled prison packs and sects of great ones
>
> That ebb and flow by the moon.
>
> **EDMUND**   Take them away.
>
> **LEAR** Upon such sacrifices, my Cordelia,
>
> The gods themselves throw incense. Have I caught thee? [*Embraces her*]
>
> He that parts us shall bring a brand from heaven,
>
> And fire us hence like foxes. Wipe thine eyes;
>
> The good-years shall devour them, flesh and fell,
>
> Ere they shall make us weep! ...

(c)   On a separate piece of paper, write a comparison of the way Lear's language changes in these two passages. Use your annotations to help you.

CONTINUED ➡

> **KEY SKILLS**
>
> **Using more than one quotation**
>
> It is often appropriate to find more than one piece of evidence or quotation to support the point you are making. This will show to the examiner that you know the play well, and will allow you to discuss structure and the development of an idea across the play.

Prose and blank verse

9   Define what you understand by the term **blank verse**.

....

....

NOTE: Check your answers before moving on to the next activity.

10   You should be aware that blank verse is a form of **poetry** and therefore could be approached and analysed in much the same way as a poem. Consider the form, shape, line breaks, patterning, variations in rhythm and sound effects such as alliteration.

Annotate the following short extract from the play as though it were a stand-alone poem. Consider the poetic devices Shakespeare has used.

> Blow winds and crack your cheeks! Rage, blow!
>
> You cataracts and hurricanoes, spout
>
> Till you have drenched our steeples, drowned the cocks!
>
> You sulphurous and thought-executing fires,
>
> Vaunt-couriers of oak-cleaving thunderbolts,
>
> Singe my white head! And thou, all-shaking thunder,
>
> Strike flat the thick rotundity o'the world,
>
> Crack nature's moulds, all germens spill at once
>
> That make ingrateful man!

11   Approximately three-quarters of *King Lear* is written in blank verse, the remainder in prose. Renaissance drama typically contained a combination of the two. Shakespeare and his contemporaries broadly followed theatrical convention in deciding whether or not to write in blank verse or prose.

Which of the following would normally be written in blank verse, and which in prose? Write **Blank verse** or **Prose** next to each item.

COMIC SCENES	*Prose*
MOMENTS OF HIGH DRAMA OR EMOTIONAL INTENSITY	
'LOW STATUS' CHARACTERS	
COURT SCENES	
LETTERS	

CONTINUED ➡

LINES SPOKEN BY ROYALTY	
'MAD' SCENES	
SOLILOQUIES	

12 Flick through your copy of *King Lear* and identify scenes and passages written in prose. Reflect on why Shakespeare has used prose at that particular point. Your answers to Question 11 may help you.

13 Typically for Shakespeare, he used his judgement about which of the above conventions he would follow and, in *King Lear*, he frequently broke the rules or was inconsistent in their application.

(a) Why are the exchanges between Edmund, Gloucester and Edgar in prose in Act 1 Scene 2?

....

....

....

(b) Why does Lear switch to prose mid-scene when talking to 'Poor Tom' in Act 3 Scene 4 lines 99 – 107?

....

....

....

(c) Why does Lear switch to blank verse in the height of his madness mid-scene in Act 4 Scene 6 lines 156–167, beginning 'Thou, rascal beadle'?

....

....

....

(d) Why is Edmund's soliloquy starting 'This is the excellent foppery of the world' in Act 1 Scene 2 in prose?

....

....

....

TAKING IT FURTHER

14 Read the passage from Act 4 Scene 6, beginning 'Is't not the King' on line 106 and ending 'it smells of mortality' on line 129. Then read the extract on the following page from a high-level student essay analysing the **language** of this passage.

CONTINUED →

Annotate the response A–E to show the strengths listed below.
A Accurate use of literary terminology
B Embedded quotations
C Purposeful reference to wider critical reading
D Purposeful consideration of the influence of contexts
E Precise analysis of quotations

Lear is, at this point, at the height of his madness. The focus of Lear's obsessive fury in this passage is, initially, on Gloucester's adultery but it soon switches to a misogynistic rant against Goneril and Regan and women in general. The passage is littered with words associated with intense fear and loathing of women's sexual desires, such as 'lecher', 'copulation', 'luxury' and 'soiled'. As throughout the play, Shakespeare here deploys bestial imagery as, 'down from the waist', women are referred to metaphorically as 'centaurs'. Lear may well be articulating Jacobean, patriarchal concerns about the emasculating effects of sexually powerful women.

Of course, Lear cannot consciously be aware of Goneril and Regan's lust for Edmund. So this is perhaps an example of what critic Maynard Mack called the 'insight' into the truth that only madness brings. Indeed, the language in this passage charts Lear's mental deterioration — his peripeteia — as Shakespeare switches, mid-speech, from blank verse to prose. Lear's language ultimately breaks down. A list outlines a hellish vision of female genitals as the source of burning sexually transmitted diseases: 'the sulphurous pit, burning, scalding, stench, consumption'. This is then followed by angry non-verbal vocalisations 'Fie' and 'pah'. These suggest Lear is struggling to articulate his ideas as well, contributing to the overall dramatic impact of an angry but impotent king.

15 Read the passage from Act 4 Scene 2, beginning 'I have been worth the whistling' on line 29 to 'O vain fool' on line 62. On a separate sheet of paper, write a similar analysis of this passage. Use the paragraphs in Question 14 as a model to help you.

Contexts

In the exam, you will need to demonstrate an understanding of 'the significance and influence of the contexts in which literary texts are written and received' (AO3). You will need to understand and explore key contexts such as the genre of tragedy and Jacobean ideas about social class, religion and madness. You should be aware of the different ways in which *King Lear* has been interpreted and understood across time. In your essays, you will also need to show how, as you develop your argument and analysis, these contexts have **influenced and shaped** the ideas and methods in the play.

STARTING OUT

1 (a) Circle the words and phrases below that you think could refer to important elements of *King Lear*'s contexts.

Gender roles	Education	Racism	Monarchy and King James
Madness	Social hierarchy	Tragedy	Science
Exploration of the 'New World'			

(b) Take **two** of your circled contexts and suggest for each how it would have influenced perceptions of the play in Shakespeare's time, and how it might influence audiences now.

CONTEXT	SHAKESPEARE'S TIME	TWENTY-FIRST CENTURY
1		
2		

DEVELOPING YOUR IDEAS

Tragedy

2 Activities in the 'Characterisation' chapter of this workbook have asked you to consider Lear as a tragic hero. The following statements could be said to describe some **general** characteristics of classical tragedy. How and to what extent could each be applied to the play *King Lear*? Explain your answer in the space provided.

(a) Tragedies end with the death of the protagonist (tragic hero), often alongside the deaths of others caught up in the events.

This applies to *King Lear* because:

....

....

....

CONTINUED ➡

(b) The tragic hero will learn something through his or her suffering and come to see the errors he or she has made.
This applies to *King Lear* because:

....

....

....

(c) The tragic hero will have a struggle for power with an antagonist (tragic villain). The antagonist will play a key role in the hero's destruction.
This applies to *King Lear* because:

....

....

....

(d) The tragic hero's actions will affect the world and people around him or her, creating chaos.
This applies to *King Lear* because:

....

....

....

(e) Language, especially poetry, is used to heighten the tragedy.
This applies to *King Lear* because:

....

....

....

(f) Fate plays a key role in a tragedy: the hero's destruction is shown to be inevitable.
This applies to *King Lear* because:

....

....

....

(g) Tragedies lead the audience to a greater understanding of the human condition.
This applies to *King Lear* because:

....

....

....

Antagonist: the character in a text whose goals are in opposition to the goals of the protagonist.
Human condition: this normally refers to the different aspects of our lives which make us human, such as childhood, growth, sex, ageing and mortality.

KEY SKILLS

King Lear and tragedy

The title of the play in the Folio text is *The Tragedy of King Lear*. The 'genre' of tragedy exerted a huge influence on the creation of the play. You should look for and analyse ways in which tragic conventions appear or have been adapted. Writing about *King Lear* as a tragedy will help you to write a high-level essay, especially for AO3 (Context).

3   Consider other tragedies you have read or seen, such as Shakespeare's *Romeo and Juliet* or *Macbeth*; Arthur Miller's *Death of a Salesman;* or perhaps Thomas Hardy's novel *Tess of the d'Urbervilles*. Do they follow the 'conventions' you considered in Question 2 in the same way as *King Lear,* or are there significant differences? Jot down some initial comparisons in the space provided below.

Challenge yourself

Why do we watch tragedies? Why watch a performance of *King Lear* where the world view is so relentlessly bleak, a character is blinded on stage and Cordelia dies unnecessarily at the end? Critic A. D. Nutall argues that modern theatre goers 'value the disturbing, the jagged, the painful' and enjoy the discomfort they feel. Do you agree? Why do people pay to watch disturbing plays and films?

King James and monarchy

4   How might the following statements about King James, his court and Jacobean ideas of monarchy have influenced *King Lear*?

(a) King James (who was crowned King of England in 1603, a couple of years before *King Lear* was written) believed passionately in his own divine right (and responsibility) to govern. He therefore expected unquestioning obedience from all his subjects. He claimed kings were 'God's lieutenants upon earth'.

....

....

....

....

(b) King James surrounded himself with flattering and ambitious courtiers, seeking favours and personal advance.

....

CONTINUED ➔

....

....

(c) King James was very profligate: he spent four times as much as Queen Elizabeth on fashionable clothing.

....

....

(d) King James's intention was to unify the two kingdoms of England and Scotland.

....

....

(e) The final years of Queen Elizabeth's reign were characterised by an anxiety over who should succeed her as sovereign because Elizabeth did not have any children.

....

....

....

Challenge yourself

We know that *King Lear* was performed before King James and his court on 26 December 1606. How do you think King James might have responded? Do you think the play criticises monarchy and the status quo, or supports it?

Jacobean society

5 (a) Listed below are four aspects of Jacobean society which probably influenced *King Lear*. Match the aspect to the quotations from *King Lear*. There may be more than one aspect for each quotation.

A   Many contemporaries of Shakespeare would have believed that God had a natural order for everything in society. This was known as the Great Chain of Being. On Earth, God created a social order for everybody and chose where you belonged. In other words, the king or queen was in charge because God put him or her there and he or she was only answerable to God. The Great Chain of Being includes everything from God and the angels at the top, to humans, then animals, with rocks and minerals at the bottom. You were a king, nobleman, or a farmer, or a beggar, because that was the place God had ordained for you.

B   Despite the prevalence of the idea of a fixed social system, political thinking was changing in Jacobean England. Social mobility was becoming a reality, as people earned wealth from commerce rather than the land. This created an emerging social class of people who were under no ancient social obligation to old feudal loyalties and instead were motivated by self-interest.

C   Poverty, unemployment and food shortages were frequent, especially in the 1590s. There were many food riots and protests, including some in Warwickshire, Shakespeare's home county. Bedlam beggars would have been a familiar sight to many in the Jacobean audience – figures who roamed the land, pleading for charity. They were either mentally ill or pretended to be so.

D   The Jacobeans had a passionate interest in justice and law. Litigation (taking someone to court, often a neighbour) was a common feature of life in Shakespeare's England. A contemporary court scandal in 1603 may have influenced Shakespeare as he wrote *King Lear*. It involved Brian Annesley, an elderly, wealthy Kentishman and two of his three daughters who tried to have their father declared insane in an attempt to take control of his estate.

CONTINUED ➔

Answers can be found at: www.hoddereducation.co.uk/workbookanswers

QUOTATION	CONTEXT A–D
ALBANY: [to EDGAR] Methought thy very gait did prophesy / A royal nobleness	A
EDGAR: The country gives me proof and precedent / Of Bedlam beggars, who, with roaring voices / Strike in their numbed and mortified bare arms / Pins, wooden pricks, nails	
EDMUND: Let me, if not by birth, have lands by wit	
LEAR: 'Tis our fast intent / To shake all cares and business from our age, / Conferring them on younger strengths	
KENT: [on OSWALD] That such a slave as this should wear a sword, / Who wears no honesty. Such smiling rogues as these / Like rats oft bite the holy cords atwain	
LEAR: Plate sin with gold, / And the strong lance of justice hurtless breaks; / Arm it in rags, a pygmy's straw does pierce it.	
LEAR: Unaccommodated man is no more but such a poor, bare, forked animal as thou art. Off, off, you lendings …	
LEAR: I'll see their trial first. Bring in their evidence. / [to EDGAR] Thou robed man of justice, take thy place.	
EDMUND: Well, then, / Legitimate Edgar, I must have your land.	
LEAR: Poor naked wretches … How shall your houseless heads and unfed sides … defend you / From seasons such as these? O, I have ta'en / Too little care of this.	
KENT: [to CORNWALL] Call not your stocks for me; I serve the King, / On whose employment I was sent to you. / You shall do small respect … Stocking his messenger.	
GENTLEMAN: [on LEAR] A sight most pitiful in the meanest wretch, / Past speaking of in a king.	

(b) The paragraph from a student essay below explores the ways in which contexts have influenced the presentation of Oswald. Underline all references to context in the paragraph.

Kent is clearly appalled by Oswald's behaviour. He calls him a 'smiling rogue' who has no honesty. Oswald represents the 'new man' of the Jacobean age, an emerging class who were motivated by self-interest. Kent confirms this in a later simile, likening Oswald to a 'rat' who bites 'the holy cords' of feudal family and community traditions apart. Oswald and Edmund are shown unsympathetically, so the play might therefore be criticising the social phenomenon of the 'new man'.

(c) Select two quotations from the table above and convert them into analytical paragraphs which take into account the influence of contexts. Use the example in Question 5(b) to help you.

(i) ....

....

....

....

....

(ii) ....

....

....

CONTINUED ➡

....

....

Performance context

6   *King Lear* has had an interesting performance history. In 1681, Nahum Tate, an Irish poet, rewrote substantial parts of *King Lear*. His version proved so popular, Shakespeare's version was not performed in full again until 1845. Some key changes Tate made include:

   (a) Cordelia does not leave for France, but stays in England and tries to find her father in the storm.

   (b) Lear and Cordelia do not die.

   (c) Cordelia and Edgar fall in love and will marry and be future monarchs.

   Why do you think Tate made the changes he did and why did they prove so popular in the eighteenth and early nineteenth centuries?

   ....

   ....

   ....

   ....

7   Critic A. C. Bradley condemned the blinding of Gloucester as a 'revolting or shocking spectacle' and as a 'blot upon *King Lear* as a stage-play'. For most of its stage history, Gloucester's blinding was performed off-stage, then it was staged with Gloucester facing away from the audience. It is only since Peter Brook's 1962 production (in which Cornwall used one of his spurs to gouge out an eye) that it has been commonly performed in full view of the audience.

   (a) What does this tell us about the different ways in which *King Lear* has been received and interpreted by audiences and directors over the years?

   ....

   ....

   ....

   (b) Imagine you have watched a version of *King Lear* in which the blinding of Gloucester was conducted off-stage. Write a message on the theatre's social media explaining why you feel it would have been better to have shown the blinding on stage.

   ....

   ....

   ....

   ....

   ....

TAKING IT FURTHER

8   Look at the following exam-style questions. On a separate piece of paper, jot down a brief essay plan for each question. For each plan, you must think about how you could include at least **two** purposeful points on the significance and influence of contexts. Write those two points in the space provided beneath each question.

   (a) **Explore the presentation of the character of Lear in *King Lear*. You must relate your discussion to relevant contextual factors.**

CONTINUED

Answers can be found at: www.hoddereducation.co.uk/workbookanswers

Context 1:

....

....

Context 2:

....

....

(b) Consider the view that Shakespeare presents the villains in *King Lear* as going against the natural social order.

Context 1:

....

....

Context 2:

....

....

(c) 'Shakespeare presents a world without justice in *King Lear*.' To what extent do you agree with this view? Remember to comment on dramatic methods.

Context 1:

....

....

Context 2:

....

....

9   The paragraph from a student essay below misses several opportunities to integrate and explore some of the contexts covered in this chapter and elsewhere. Rewrite it, making the relevance of context clear.

Edmund is established as an outsider at the beginning of the play, as Gloucester describes his son as a 'knave' who 'came somewhat saucily to the world before he was sent for'. Possibly as revenge for the way his father has treated him, Edmund sets out to rise through the social hierarchy and ultimately usurp his own father as Duke of Gloucester.

....

....

....

....

....

KEY SKILLS

Integrating contexts

Referencing contextual factors is only valuable when it genuinely informs your interpretation of *King Lear*. Contextual material which is clumsily 'bolted on' will contribute little to your argument.

Critical approaches

A successful student of literature will understand that texts can be read and interpreted differently: there is no 'fixed' meaning in a literary text. This section will draw your attention to the different ways in which *King Lear* can be read and understood.

STARTING OUT

1 **LEAR**   I am a man

   More sinned against than sinning.

   (a) How do you interpret these lines (from Act 3 Scene 2 lines 59–60)?

   ....

   ....

   ....

   (b) Read these seven different interpretations of the same quotation. Circle two which you feel are the most convincing and/or interesting.

This remark is Lear at his self-pitying worst. Lear seems to be unable to admit his own shortcomings or realise the gods are punishing him for his error of judgement.	This is an important signpost in Lear's journey towards 'seeing clearly'. He has already acknowledged his mistake in Act 1 Scene 5: 'I did her wrong' and that he has sinned himself.	These lines confirm that Lear's suffering is essentially spiritual: his inner world is one of sin, guilt and retribution.

   Lear is simply wrong here. He has committed more sins than had sins committed against him.

Lear rightly feels that his suffering at the hands of his daughters is inappropriately harsh.	Shakespeare is here locating the play in a determinedly Christian universe; Lear is using the language of Christianity, with echoes of the Bible.	This quotation cannot be read out of its immediate context: it concludes a long speech in which Lear calls upon the storm to reveal all hidden crimes and sins of humanity, including his own. Lear's next lines are expressions of concern for the Fool.

   (c) Has your own interpretation changed as a result of completing Question 1(b)? Do you read Lear's words differently now?

   ....

   ....

   ....

   ....

KEY SKILLS

More than one interpretation

Question 1 should have brought into sharper focus the idea that literary texts can be read in more than one way. For many AS/A-level English Literature courses, you will need to have an awareness of other interpretations (AO5) and, as Question 1(c) indicated, you also need to show how they influence your **own** argument.

DEVELOPING YOUR IDEAS

Traditional criticism

2 Pre-twentieth-century critics recognised the power of *King Lear* but frequently questioned what they saw as the play's gratuitous violence.

   (a) The writer Samuel Johnson, writing in 1765, found Cordelia's death at the end to be 'contrary to the natural ideas of justice'. What do you think Johnson meant by 'natural ideas of justice'?

   ....

   ....

   (b) What is your response to the ending? Why did Shakespeare unnecessarily, it seems, have Cordelia die at the end? Surely the Gentleman dispatched to save her could have got there in time?

   ....

   ....

   ....

   ....

   (c) Now read carefully the following extract from critic Fintan O'Toole's *King Lear: Zero Hour*, in which he argues that the play deliberately upsets all comfortable and traditional assumptions, such as justice, morality and loyalty.

   > The story bursts out beyond the moral ending of the play, the overwhelming sense of injustice breaks through the even balancing of good and evil. And this isn't a failure of the play: it is the whole point of the play's structure.
   >
   > There is no simple sense of morality – of what is virtue and what is vice – in *King Lear* ... Does *King Lear* endorse morality or deny it? It does neither: it shows morality falling apart under the stress of the play's traumatic events and emotions.

   Look again at your own response to Question 2(b). Are you now able to add to it in any way as a result of reading this extract from O'Toole?

KEY SKILLS

Evaluating criticism

It is acceptable, even encouraged, to question or interrogate critics' interpretations. Try to evaluate their ideas and use them, ultimately, to build your own argument.

3 Russian novelist Leo Tolstoy famously launched a withering attack on *King Lear*. On a separate piece of paper, write a short speech for a classroom debate in which you argue that *King Lear* is a terrible play, not worthy of study. Make reference to at least two of Tolstoy's points listed here:
   - He hated the Fool, saying he serves no purpose and makes jokes which are not funny.
   - It is completely unbelievable that Edgar should run away so easily and with hardly any evidence.
   - Lear's speeches are dismissed by Tolstoy as unnatural.
   - Lear's argument against injustice in Act 4 Scene 6 is out of place in the mouth of an insane man.
   - In the final scene, we feel ashamed at Lear's final speech in the same way we might feel ashamed at a bad joke.

4 Romantic critics of the early nineteenth century found plot deficiencies as well, but they also praised the 'poetry' of the play. Poet Percy Shelley wrote that the play is 'the most perfect specimen of dramatic poetry existing in the world'. Choose your favourite speech from the play. Select three aspects of the speech to support Shelley's view.

CONTINUED →

(i) ....

....

(ii) ....

....

(iii) ....

....

Challenge yourself

John Keats, another Romantic writer, wrote a sonnet called 'On Sitting Down to Read King Lear Once Again'. In it, he chooses to put away a pleasantly light, 'serene' book and instead pick up his copy of *King Lear*:

> ... for once again the fierce dispute,
>
> Betwixt damnation and impassion'd clay
>
> Must I burn through; once more humbly assay
>
> The bitter-sweet of this Shakespearian fruit.
>
> ... when I am consumed in the fire,
>
> Give me new Phoenix wings to fly at my desire.

What is Keats suggesting here about the impact and experience of reading *King Lear*?

Sonnet: A 14-line poem written in iambic pentameter and with an intricate rhyme scheme.

Political criticism

5   A political approach to criticism claims that literary texts cannot be separated from their social and historical contexts. They look at ways in which texts support or question prevailing contextual ideas or ideologies, specifically those related to political power and economics. Marxist critics will also look at the representation of those who own wealth, power and capital as well as those who are poor or disenfranchised.

(a) How are the poor represented in the play?

....

....

....

(b) When Lear is on the heath, what does he learn about poverty?

....

....

....

 CONTINUED

Answers can be found at: www.hoddereducation.co.uk/workbookanswers

(c) Read Lear's speech to Gloucester in Act 4 Scene 6, beginning 'Thou, rascal beadle' on line 156 and ending 'things thou dost not' on line 169. What is Lear saying about justice and the law, and power and corruption here?

....

....

....

....

....

6 Critic Jonathan Dollimore claims that Shakespeare actively questions and subverts contemporary political power and ideology. *King Lear* exposes the injustices and inequalities of Jacobean society. Lear's identity is shown to be not 'divinely' given, but rooted in family and authority. When he loses both, he loses his mind. Answer the following questions to refine your understanding of Dollimore's position.

(a) Where does Lear's initial authority actually come from in the play? Look at Act 1 Scene 1.

....

....

(b) What problems with inheritance does the play highlight?

....

....

....

(c) How do most of the 'noble' men and women in the play behave?

....

....

....

(d) Is there a total collapse of governance and authority by the end of the play?

....

....

7 Leonard Tennenhouse, although a 'political' critic like Dollimore, completely disagrees with Dollimore's reading of the play. He argues that *King Lear* demonstrates the dangers of *not* following the established patriarchal hierarchy. The play affirms and legitimises oppressive structures of power. Answer the following questions to refine your understanding of Tennenhouse's position.

(a) What are the consequences of Lear's refusal to govern as (divinely appointed) king in Act 1 Scene 1? Could this be viewed as a warning?

....

....

....

....

(b) Now that they no longer have any legitimacy or state power, how do Lear's royal knights behave in Acts 1 and 2?

....

....

(c) What crime against aristocratic laws of family and inheritance does Gloucester commit? How is he punished?

....

....

....

(d) In what ways is the established order, the status quo, re-established in Act 4? Consider the relationships between Gloucester and Edgar, Gloucester and Lear and Lear and Cordelia.

....

....

....

(e) How does the eventual ruler of Britain (Edgar) view monarchy and ideas of family and loyalty? How might this be significant for Tennenhouse's interpretation?

....

....

....

8 Which of these two views – Dollimore and Tennenhouse – do you agree with more and why?

....

....

....

....

....

....

....

Challenge yourself

Even ideas and interpretations of what constitutes a tragedy are not fixed, and political critics have some very interesting views on the ways in which tragedies embody the structures and tensions of power. Shakespearean scholar J. W. Lever, in his influential book *The Tragedy of the State*, provides an alternative reading of the tragic hero. Lear's downfall is not brought about by some fatal tragic flaw – by his own 'blindness', for example; rather, the flaw is in the world he inhabits: the 'political state, the social order it upholds'. Do you agree? Are the deaths, devastation and catastrophes brought about by a problem with the feudal monarchical system, rather than Lear's own errors of judgement?

Feminist criticism

9   Feminist critics are interested in the representation of women in literature. They highlight, criticise and resist the patriarchal assumptions and gendered stereotypes in a text. Some feminist critics think *King Lear* questions patriarchy and exposes it as vicious and unjust. Other feminist critics argue that *King Lear* presents a conventional male view of the world in which Goneril and Regan are demonised.

Think carefully about each statement in the table below and consider how far you agree (10 = agree the most).

(a)

STATEMENT ON THE PLAY FROM A FEMINIST PERSPECTIVE	DO YOU AGREE?
A Lear is a patriarchal figure: he treats his daughters as subordinates who must obey him.	/10
B The play is filled with male disgust with female sexuality.	/10
C Lear's daughters' defiance and resistance are shown in the play as going against the natural order of things.	/10
D Lear regards Cordelia as a piece of property, to be disposed of as he sees fit.	/10
E Goneril and Regan are justified in their resistance to their father's behaviour.	/10
F The play confirms male stereotypes of women: the demonised seductress (Goneril and Regan) and the virginal saint (Cordelia).	/10
G Lear progresses towards the feminine in the play: he learns to weep and to adopt an 'equal' relationship with Cordelia.	/10
H In *King Lear*, the feminine must either submit (Cordelia) or be destroyed (Goneril and Regan).	/10

(b) Identify which of the above statements you agreed with the most and explain why.

....

....

....

(c) Identify which of the above statements you disagreed with the most and explain why.

....

....

....

(d) Did reading any of the statements change or make you question your own ideas about *King Lear*?

....

....

....

Challenge yourself

What do you think is the significance of Lear (and Gloucester) having no wife? What impact do you imagine a wife would have had on the play?

10 Read the short passage from Act 1 Scene 4, beginning 'Are you our daughter' (line 209) and ending 'Make servants of their betters' (line 248). Think about how a feminist critic might respond to the passage and then answer the following questions.

   (a) What is Goneril concerned about here? Do you feel her concerns are justifiable?

   ....

   ....

   ....

   ....

   (b) Look at the way Goneril uses language in the longer speech, beginning line 228 'This admiration, sir'. Is she shown as being dominant here or do you think she is trying to be respectful and polite in her request?

   ....

   ....

   ....

   ....

   (c) What is Lear implying about Goneril when he says 'Are you our daughter?' and 'I should be false persuaded I had daughters'? Why does he interpret her behaviour as being unnatural?

   ....

   ....

   ....

   ....

   (d) Look again at the way Lear responds in his speech, lines 243–246. What does Lear think of his daughter? Do you think his response is reasonable?

   ....

   ....

   ....

   ....

   (e) Do you think the play is encouraging us to agree with Lear that Goneril is a 'devil' and an evil character? Or is it more complex than this?

   ....

   ....

   ....

   ....

   ....

Challenge yourself

Feminist critic Carol Rutter, in her essay 'Eel Pie and Ugly Sisters in *King Lear*', explores the relationship in the play between language and female power. Find evidence to support some of Rutter's points below:

- Lear's 'tears of impotent rage are indeed the sign of the female'.
- Lear's 'cursing is the language of political exclusion … Women curse. They curse because they cannot act … Lear, cursing, is one of them'.
- Goneril and Regan 'assume the male voice, the male space Lear abandons'.
- Lear struggles to speak on a number of occasions in the play: 'His words fail' him.

TAKING IT FURTHER

11 Read the passage from Act 4 Scene 6, beginning 'Thou must be patient' (line 174) and ending 'Past speaking of in a king' (line 201). Look again at your answers to the activities in the 'Political Criticism' section. Write two paragraphs on a separate piece of paper, from a political perspective, on how Lear is being presented in this passage. You could consider:

- Lear's ideas about the 'great stage of fools' as a comment on Jacobean society
- Lear's views on kingship
- Lear's madness and murderous thoughts
- the way the Gentleman talks to Lear.

12 Read the passage from Act 2 Scene 4, beginning 'Now I prithee, daughter' (line 407) and ending 'And in good time you gave it' (line 439). Look again at your answers to the activities in the 'Feminist Criticism' section. Write two paragraphs on a separate piece of paper, from a feminist perspective, on how Goneril and Regan are being presented in this passage. You could consider:

- Lear's cursing and descriptions of Goneril
- Regan's use of language as she bargains with Lear
- Regan's interruption of Lear
- Goneril and Regan's position of authority and control.

Boosting your skills

This section will focus on how you can approach different types of question you might encounter in the exam. Subsequent activities will go on to develop and refine your essay-writing skills.

Tackling question types

1   Draw a line to match the skills with the AS/A-level English Literature Assessment Objectives. There may be more than one skill for each Assessment Objective.

A	The accuracy and fluency of your writing	AO1
B	Demonstrating an awareness that there is more than one way to interpret the play	
C	Making links between the play and another literary text	AO2
D	Creating and developing an argument and a clear structure	
E	Showing an understanding of the importance and influence of contexts	AO3
F	Using literary terms and concepts	
G	Allowing other readings – including those from critics or statements given in the exam – to influence your own interpretation	AO4
H	Analysing meanings and how they are shaped by language	
I	Showing an understanding that the play can be understood differently by audiences and readers over time	AO5

2   Either from your own class notes or from your own research, find a past exam question from the exam board you are studying and write it below. NOTE: some *King Lear* exam questions have two distinct parts to them, or may appear in more than one section in the exam.

....

....

....

KEY SKILLS

The importance of the Assessment Objectives

Ensure you know which of the Assessment Objectives apply to the question you will be answering in the exam or for your Non-Examined Assessment (coursework). There will be important differences between exam boards and specifications and also, in some cases, between the AS and the A-level exams.

DEVELOPING YOUR IDEAS

You will encounter different types of exam questions, depending on the course you are studying. You may also be studying *King Lear* for the Non-Examined Assessment component (coursework).

General questions about the whole play

3   For example:

Explore how Shakespeare presents X in *King Lear*. You must relate your discussion to relevant contextual factors and ideas from your critical reading.

'X' here could be a theme/idea; character/relationship; or distinctive literary/dramatic technique or approach (such as 'imagery'). Importantly, your response will need to range across the whole play.

(a) Write your own essay question on a **theme** in the play.

....

....

(b) Write your own question on a **significant dramatic or literary technique** in the play.

....

....

(c) Write your own essay question on a **significant relationship between two characters** in the play.

....

....

(d) For each of the above questions, select **three** key passages, speeches or scenes which you could refer to in your response.

Questions which invite you to respond to a viewpoint or statement

4   These questions will contain an interpretation of a particular aspect of the play, such as character, theme or structure. You will need to provide your own take on the given statement, which could involve agreeing completely, disagreeing completely or a combination of the two. You may find that you agree with some aspects of the statement, but not all.

For example:

'We cannot sympathise with Lear.' To what extent do you agree with this view? Remember to include in your answer relevant comment on Shakespeare's dramatic methods.

(a) What are the differences between this type of question and the questions you looked at in Question 3? How should you approach these two types of question differently?

....

....

....

CONTINUED ➡

(b) Look at the following views on the play. For each statement, put an 'x' on the agree/disagree scale. Go on to explain why you placed the 'x' where you did.

A 'Pity and mercy are words without a meaning' in *King Lear* (Swinburne)

Completely disagree	put an 'x' on the line	Completely agree

Explanation of my answer:

....

....

....

....

B There is a 'sinister humour at the heart of this play' (Wilson Knight)

Completely disagree	put an 'x' on the line	Completely agree

Explanation of my answer:

....

....

....

....

C *King Lear* is about 'power, property and inheritance' (Dollimore)

Completely disagree	put an 'x' on the line	Completely agree

Explanation of my answer:

....

....

....

....

D 'The motivation of the sisters [Goneril and Regan] lies not in what Lear has done to them but in what they are: evil' (Mack)

Completely disagree	put an 'x' on the line	Completely agree

Explanation of my answer:

....

....

....

....

CONTINUED ➡

E 'The Fool's only purpose is to provide comic relief to the main tragedy of the play'

Completely disagree	.... put an 'x' on the line	Completely agree

Explanation of my answer:

....

....

....

....

....

Questions which ask you to analyse a passage from King Lear

5 Some questions will ask you to closely analyse the passage with a particular focus (such as 'the presentation of Edmund in the extract'). Others will ask you to explore the significance of the extract to the tragedy of the play as a whole.

Read the following exam question and the accompanying extract carefully. Then annotate the passage with some points you could consider in an essay. Use some of the following prompts to help you.

AO2 Analysis of language and meanings
- Examples of repetition and patterning
- Imagery of animals, torture and suffering
- Stage directions (including implied)
- Rhyme

AO3 The influence of contexts
- Jacobean attitudes towards monarchy and the Great Chain of Being
- Attitudes towards legitimacy and illegitimacy
- Varying attitudes towards death
- God, religion and justice

AO4 Comparing literary texts
- The tragic death of the tragic hero
- Sadness and pity (pathos); catharsis
- Lear's changing tragic stature
- A renewed hope at the end of a tragedy
- A sense of a 'lesson being learnt' from the catastrophe

AO5 Awareness of different interpretations
- Is the devastating ending necessary?
- Can some comfort be derived from the extract?
- Views and attitudes towards Lear as a tragic figure
- Reactions to Kent's refusal to reign and welcoming death

Read the extract on the following page. Explore the significance of this extract in relation to the tragedy of the play as a whole. Remember to include in your answer relevant analysis of Shakespeare's dramatic methods.

CONTINUED →

LEAR   And my poor fool is hanged. No, no, no life!

Why should a dog, a horse, a rat, have life,

And thou no breath at all? O thou'lt come no more,

Never, never, never, never, never!

Pray you, undo this button: thank you, sir.

Do you see this? Look on her: look, her lips,

Look there, look there! [*He dies*]

EDGAR   He faints: my lord, my lord!

KENT   Break, heart, I prithee break.

EDGAR   Look up, my lord.

KENT   Vex not his ghost: O, let him pass. He hates him

That would upon the rack of this tough world

Stretch him out longer.

EDGAR   O he is gone, indeed.

KENT   The wonder is, he hath endured so long;

He but usurped his life.

ALBANY   Bear them from hence. Our present business

Is general woe. [*To KENT and EDGAR*] Friends of my soul, you twain

Rule in this realm and the gored state sustain.

KENT   I have a journey, sir, shortly to go;

My master calls me, I must not say no.

EDGAR   The weight of this sad time we must obey;

Speak what we feel, not what we ought to say.

The oldest hath borne most; we that are young

Shall never see so much, nor live so long.

[*Exeunt, with a dead march*]

Essay planning and structure

STARTING OUT

1 The statements below are about what to do when **planning** an essay in the exam. Circle the statements that are **not** likely to help you to write a successful essay on *King Lear*.

NOTE: Make sure you check your answers before proceeding to the subsequent activities.

A Spend no more than two minutes planning – it is more important that you use the time writing a five page essay.

B Read the question carefully a number of times and underline key words and phrases.

C Consider the order you can make your points – can one point lead on clearly to another?

D If you have a choice of questions, read both questions carefully – don't just go with your initial instinct.

E Spend the planning time trying to remember how you wrote your recent A-grade mock essay on a similar topic.

F Do not worry about having a central argument – hopefully you will have thought of one by the time you write your conclusion.

G For each point, think about the evidence/ quotations you can use to support it.

DEVELOPING YOUR IDEAS

Reading the question

2 It is very important that you spend time in the exam reading the question carefully and working out what exactly it is asking you to do.

Read this example of a 'responding to a statement' exam question and answer the questions that follow.

'Edmund is no more than a cruel and ambitious villain.' To what extent do you agree with this view? Remember to include in your answer relevant analysis of Shakespeare's dramatic methods.

(a) What do 'cruel and ambitious' mean?

....

....

(b) How could the words 'cruel and ambitious' relate to Edmund?

....

....

(c) Why do you think the question includes 'no more than'? What could this be guiding you towards?

....

....

(d) What is 'To what extent do you agree' asking you to do?

....

....

CONTINUED ➡

(e) What is meant by 'dramatic methods'?

....

....

3 Look at the following two exam questions and highlight and annotate them as you might in the exam. Use the approaches and questions in Question 2 to help you.

Explore how Shakespeare presents suffering in *King Lear*. You must relate your discussion to relevant contextual factors and ideas from your critical reading.

Consider the view that 'the characters in *King Lear* inhabit a world without justice'.

Planning your response

4 You may find a particular approach to planning essays more effective than other approaches. Try these two activities to see which works best for you.

(a) **'Edmund is no more than a cruel and ambitious villain.' To what extent do you agree with this view? Remember to include in your answer relevant comment on Shakespeare's dramatic methods.**

Create a spider diagram with different points you could make in response to this question.

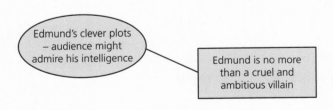

(b) **Examine the view that 'Goneril and Regan are heartless villains and deserve no sympathy at all.'**

On a separate piece of paper, list points you could make in response to this question. An example has been provided for you, below.

Play condemns them in the imagery used – predatory animals – 'detested kite', 'wolvish visage'

CONTINUED ➜

(c) Which of the two approaches to planning did you prefer and why?

....

....

....

5   You should consider asking yourself the following general questions when planning a response to a question on a passage from *King Lear*.

●   What is the passage's place in the development of plot? How does it fit within the tragedy as a whole? What has just happened? How are future events being prepared or foreshadowed?

●   What does the section reveal about characters?

●   How far might the extract introduce or develop one or more of the play's themes?

●   How far does the section illustrate typical aspects of language and imagery? How do they enhance the overall meaning of the passage and the play as a whole?

●   How far does the section illustrate typical aspects of other dramatic methods? How do they enhance the overall meaning of the passage and the play as a whole?

●   What is the overall dramatic impact of the section? How is an audience likely to respond?

Read the passage from Act 5 Scene 1 of *King Lear*, line 5 'Our sister's man' to line 38 'I will go'. On a separate piece of paper, jot down some answers to the questions above. You will then have produced an essay plan for a question on this passage.

6   (a) Look again at your spider diagram for Question 4(a). There is, of course, no set number of points you need or are advised to make in an exam essay for AS/A-level English Literature, but up to five or six good, developed points can often be sufficient. If you have made more points than this in your spider diagram, see if any are weak, lack potential for development or could perhaps be combined.

(b) Look at these five points a student has selected for an essay exploring how suffering is presented in *King Lear*. What do you think would make the best order? Consider points which might link together in some way, or which develop from each other. You could also provide two contrasting views, one after the other. Number the points 1 to 5.

(A) *Lear suffers mentally and physically in the storm: he is cold, desolate and increasingly insane.*   ☐

(B) *Lear suffers at the hands of Goneril and Regan, who mistreat Kent, seek to reduce Lear's knights and ultimately cast him out into the storm.*   ☐

(C) *Gloucester's suffering parallels Lear's: both characters' torments are a necessary part of their journey towards understanding and forgiveness.*   ☐

(D) *Lear suffers when he witnesses the cruel and unjust death of his daughter.*   ☐

(E) *Lear's tragic suffering is presented as a punishment for his catastrophic error of judgement in the opening scene.*   ☐

(c) Now look at the points you identified for Questions 4(a) and 5(a). Think about the order you will present them in. Consider points which might link together in some way, or which develop from each other. You could also provide two contrasting views, one after the other. You may want to check your answers to Questions 5(b) to help you. Number your points in the order in which you now wish to make them.

(d) For each point, write down (on a separate piece of paper) the supporting evidence/quotations you will include in the essay and, where relevant, references to contexts and/or critical ideas.

KEY SKILLS

Linking your points

There are a number of ways in which you can link paragraphs. Using markers such as 'on the other hand' and 'in a similar way' can be very effective ways to begin paragraphs.

If you carry on an idea into a second paragraph, you could begin with 'Moreover, Lear's suffering can also be seen in ...'

You could challenge the preceding paragraph by starting with 'On the other hand, this view of suffering can be challenged by a feminist perspective ...'

Thinking about your argument and writing the introduction

7 'Edmund is no more than a cruel and ambitious villain.' To what extent do you agree with this view? Remember to include in your answer relevant comment on Shakespeare's dramatic methods.

(a) You have so far spent some time thinking about and planning a response to this question on Edmund. What is **your** view? Do you think Edmund is nothing more than a cruel and ambitious villain?

....

....

....

KEY SKILLS

Having an argument

AO1 states that you are being assessed on your ability to demonstrate a 'personal' response to *King Lear*. Examiners note that a marked feature of top-level responses is having a clear and consistent argument, established in the opening paragraph, sustained and developed in the main body of the essay and revisited in the conclusion.

(b) Read the introductory paragraph from a student's essay and outline beneath it three ways it could be improved.

Yes, I totally agree with this obviously accurate view on Edmund. He is clearly a cruel and ambitious character throughout the play. In this essay, I am going to look at how he is cruel and ambitious, such as the way he treats his father and the way he manipulates Goneril and Regan's affections.

(i) ....

....

(ii) ....

....

(iii) ....

....

(c) Your response to Question 6(a) may well work as an effective introduction in its own right. Read it again and make sure you are not making the same mistakes as the student in Question 6(b). If necessary, on a separate piece of paper, write it out again with any required improvements and additions.

Challenge yourself

A high-grade response might, if appropriate, be able to **integrate** an important **context** or **critical perspective** in the argument/opening paragraph. Write an introduction to the Edmund question with this in mind. You could, for example, consider Machiavellian villains or a political reading of Edmund as a radical outsider seeking to disrupt the conventional order.

Concluding

8 (a) Read the three statements below about writing conclusions. Circle those you believe to be true.

> A   The conclusion needs to be long.

> B   The conclusion should correlate in some way with your argument.

> C   The essay can end with a flourish – a compelling end to your essay.

(b) Listed below are a number of different ways to conclude an essay on *King Lear*. How you conclude will depend on the Assessment Objectives being examined for your course. Some of these methods may well be combined as well.

- Ending with a compelling quotation from the play or the critic that makes the reader think, such as 'The wheel is come full circle'; or perhaps a quotation from a critic you have learnt: 'As Arnold Kettle states, Edmund is "the new man of the incipient bourgeois revolution, the private enterprise man, the individualist go-getter."'
- Ending with a twist: present a stark, interesting alternative view from the one you have been expressing in the rest of the essay.
- Confirming why you think Edmund (or the theme, issue, or technique under discussion) is fundamental to the play.
- Provide a balanced overview of the main points you have made.
- Mentioning how audiences in Jacobean England might have responded differently from a twenty-first-century audience.
- Returning to points and phrases you made in your introduction – this often gives the essay a satisfying cohesion.

Select one of the above methods (or perhaps a combination of two) and write your conclusion to the question you have been planning in this section: '**Edmund is no more than a cruel and ambitious villain.' To what extent do you agree with this view?**

....
....
....
....
....
....
....
....
....
....
....
....
....

TAKING IT FURTHER

9 The preceding activities adopted the following approach to planning an essay on the play as a whole:

(a) If you have a choice of questions, read them both carefully before deciding.

(b) Reflect upon, underline and annotate the question to ensure you are really clear what you are being asked to do.

(c) Create a spider diagram or a list of potential points you could make to answer the question.

(d) Select the points you want to make; be prepared to discard repeated or less successful points.

(e) Think about and jot down evidence/quotations, key passages, context and, where relevant, critical viewpoints and perspectives.

(f) Decide on the order of points.

(g) Refine and confirm what your core argument is going to be; this may well end up being part of your introduction.

(h) Check to ensure all points clearly answer the question.

Now, on a separate piece of paper, follow this structure as you plan one or both of the following exam questions. Complete points (a)–(h) above in no more than **20 minutes** for each question.

A **Explore Shakespeare's use of imagery in** *King Lear.* **You must relate your discussion to relevant contextual factors and ideas from your critical reading.**

B **Consider the view that** *King Lear* **presents the triumph of good over evil.**

Essay-writing skills

STARTING OUT

1 Read the paragraph below, taken from an essay on the characterisation of Kent. Find at least three ways in which this student could improve her essay writing. Focus on the way she has written the paragraph, rather than the content.

In king lear Kent is shown to be a loyal character and contrasts with other characters such as Edmund and Goneril. 'Royal Lear, whom I have ever honoured as my king, loved as my father, as my master followed, as my great patron thought on in my prayers'. Kent is saying here that he is loyal to the king. This contrasts with other characters such as Edmund who is disloyal to his father as he seeks to gain power of his own by lying to Gloucester about Edgar and then informing on his own father to Cornwall.

(i) ....

....

(ii) ....

....

(iii) ....

....

DEVELOPING YOUR IDEAS

Quoting effectively

2   Listed below are some tips on how to quote effectively in your essays.

- Quotations should be relevant to the point you are making.
- Quotations should be brief – they can often be single words or phrases. It is rarely necessary to quote consecutive lines of dialogue.
- Quotations should be integrated into your sentence: 'Lear tells Cordelia that they will "sing like birds i'the cage" when they are in prison together.'
- It is often useful to include who says the quotation, who they are speaking to and, possibly, where (broadly) it appears in the play: 'Moments after Lear's defeat in battle, Edgar tells Gloucester to "endure" his suffering and advises him that "ripeness is all".'
- Try to include quotations you can subsequently analyse and explore (there are activities on analysing later on in this section).

Use the following quotations to illustrate the given points. Ensure, where possible, you adhere to the advice given in the list above.

(a) **Point**: Lear, in his pride, banishes Kent.

   Evidence: 'Out of my sight!'

....

....

....

(b) **Point**: Lear admits his own shortcomings and that he has made errors.

   Evidence: 'I am a very foolish, fond old man'

....

....

....

(c) **Point**: Lear calls on the storm to destroy the world.

   Evidence:

> ... spout
> Till you have drenched our steeples, drowned the cocks!
> You sulphurous and thought-executing fires,
> Vaunt-couriers of oak-cleaving thunderbolts,
> Singe my white head!

....

....

....

KEY SKILLS

Long quotations?

On the rare occasions where you find you do need to quote two or more consecutive lines of dialogue, you should write them out as a separate paragraph, without quotation marks:

CORDELIA: Nothing, my lord

LEAR: Nothing?

CORDELIA: Nothing.

You should then continue with your essay in the paragraph beneath the quotation.

Integrating contexts

3   A common error is to 'bolt on' context, either in a clumsy paragraph of its own or perhaps tacked on to the end of an analytical paragraph without any reference to the point being made. Try to integrate contextual references so they form part of your analysis.

Read these two extracts from student essays on the presentation of Edgar in *King Lear*. Annotate what you think are their good and bad points. Which do you think explores the influence of contextual factors more effectively? Write an 'examiner' comment beneath each one.

(a) From an essay on the presentation of Edgar

Due to the Machiavellian plots of his half-brother, Edgar must assume the role of a 'Bedlam beggar' to evade identification and capture. In yet another contribution to the play's motif of clothing and disguise, Edgar must 'grime with filth' and present his 'nakedness' to the 'winds and persecutions of the sky'. In the topsy-turvy world of the play, the nobleman Edgar is humiliated and becomes the 'basest and most poorest shape'. Bedlam beggars would have been a familiar sight to many in Shakespeare's audience, especially during the poverty and food shortages of the 1590s. Bedlam beggars would wander and 'enforce their charity' with pretended lunacy or prayers. Unlike, perhaps, a modern audience, Jacobeans may well have reflected on the remarkable social significance of a nobleman like Edgar being reduced to such a 'base' state.

....

....

....

....

....

....

(b) From an essay closely exploring the significance of Act 1 Scene 1 lines 35–86 to the tragedy of the play as a whole.

In what is perhaps the most significant action in all of King Lear, Lear announces that he is to relinquish all power as king. He will 'shake all cares and business' from his age and be king in name alone. King James was crowned King of England in 1603, a couple of years before King Lear was written. He was also earlier

CONTINUED ➡

Answers can be found at: www.hoddereducation.co.uk/workbookanswers

crowned King James VI of Scotland in 1567, succeeding Mary, Queen of Scots. King James I believed passionately in his own divine right (and responsibility) to rule. He therefore expected unquestioning obedience from all his subjects. He claimed kings were 'God's lieutenants upon earth, and sit upon God's throne' and that 'even by God himself they are called gods'. Kings were chosen by God and would rule as such; they would therefore, effectively, have no choice in the matter.

....

....

....

....

....

....

Analysing the ways meanings are shaped

4   For all exam question types, you will need to demonstrate to the examiner that you are able to analyse the ways in which meanings are created in *King Lear*. This will require you to conduct some close analysis of the effects of language choices, dramatic techniques and structure.

(a) Read the following short extract from *King Lear* (Act 1 Scene 4 lines 251–264). Annotate it with the following language choices and dramatic techniques:
   ● invocations
   ● images of animals and monsters
   ● other similes and metaphors
   ● repetition
   ● stage directions.

LEAR   Ingratitude, thou marble-hearted fiend,

More hideous when thou show'st thee in a child

Than the sea-monster.

ALBANY   Pray, sir, be patient.

LEAR [*to Goneril*]   Detested kite, thou liest.

My train are men of choice and rarest parts

That all particulars of duty know,

And in the most exact regards support

CONTINUED ➤

> The worships of their name. O most small fault,
>
> How ugly didst thou in Cordelia show,
>
> Which like an engine wrenched my frame of nature
>
> From the fixed place, drew from my heart all love
>
> And added to the gall. O Lear, Lear, Lear!
>
> [*striking his head*] Beat at this gate that let thy folly in
>
> And thy dear judgement out.

(b) In the extract below, a student is analysing the use of invocations in the passage. Complete the gaps with either quotations from the passage or analysis of your own.

Lear characteristically uses a number of invocations in this passage. He initially invokes 'ingratitude'. He calls it a '.................................' and uses imagery when he says it is more hideous than '....................'. This invocation therefore suggests ....

.... Later in the same passage, Lear even invokes himself in the remarkable tripling of '..,' as he criticises his own actions. He is, in a crucial, tragic moment of clarity, acknowledging what the Fool and Kent have been trying to tell him: ....

....

....

(c) Look again at the completed paragraph for Question 4(b). Identify where you (and the student) have:
- considered literary or dramatic techniques and terms
- embedded quotations
- analysed the techniques and/or the quotations.

(d) Using the completed paragraph for Question 4(b) as a model, write your own paragraph on Shakespeare's use of **figurative devices** in the passage (imagery, metaphor and/or similes).

....

....

....

....

....

....

....

....

Essay practice

STARTING OUT

1   What do you find most difficult when writing essays on *King Lear*?

....

....

DEVELOPING YOUR IDEAS

Responding to a general question about the whole play

2   General questions about the whole play could be on themes/ideas, characters or relationships, or distinctive literary or dramatic techniques, such as Shakespeare's use of setting.

Explore Shakespeare's presentation of sight and blindness in *King Lear*. You must relate your discussion to relevant contextual factors and ideas from your critical reading.

The following paragraph is extracted from a student response to this question. Answer the questions which follow. The question letters correspond with the letters in square brackets in the extract. You could refer to previous activities in this section of the workbook to help you.

The play's preoccupation with metaphorical blindness finds a physical embodiment in king lear [a]: the blinding of Gloucester. 'Pluck out his eyes!' [b] It is Goneril who originally suggests the sadistic blinding of Gloucester. During the blinding scene, Cornwall says: 'upon these eyes of thine I'll set my foot' [b]. He also says 'Out, vile jelly, [c] Where is thy lustre now?' [d] This scene has been performed differently over time. From the eighteenth century to the 1960s, this scene was either cut or the blinding was performed off stage. Only relatively recently have directors decided to include it. [e]

(a) Write the title of the play correctly.

....

(b) How could this student improve the way he has presented his evidence?

....

....

....

(c) How are line breaks in poetry indicated in literary essays?

....

(d) The student has not analysed the quotations. Add in some analysis, using at least one literary term.

....

....

....

(e) This student would be rewarded for this reference to changing contexts of reception. How could it be improved or developed?

....

....

....

CONTINUED ➔

3 (a) Read the extract from a high-level response and identify **three** things the student is doing well. Try to focus on the **way** the essay is written, rather than the content.

Explore Shakespeare's presentation of madness in *King Lear*. You must relate your discussion to relevant contextual factors and ideas from your critical reading.

When he has lost his mind, Lear's speeches appear nonsensical. They are disjointed, the references are often obscure and the topics frequently change. However, as critic Maynard Mack argues, madness also seems to give Lear a special insight and a freedom to speak the truth, in particular about corruption of the Jacobean social system. There is clear evidence of this in Act 4, in Lear's reunion with Gloucester. He tells the blinded Gloucester to 'look with thine ears' in order to understand how a corrupt judge 'rails upon yon simple thief'.

Shakespeare goes on to use the motif of animal imagery, as justice and authority is likened to a 'farmer's dog' barking 'at a beggar'. This image reduces figures of pomp and authority to a bestial state. Lear's madness has enabled him to 'see' the corrupt world for what it is. This is possibly also an oblique reference King James's court, which was notoriously associated with corrupt sycophants. Maynard Mack goes on to say that Shakespeare was able to risk this rather dangerous satire because he puts it in the mouth of an ostensibly 'mad' character.

(i) ....

....

....

(ii) ....

....

....

(iii) ....

....

....

(b) Using Question 3(a) as a model, write the 'next' paragraph from the same essay on madness. The paragraph should be a point on Lear's 'furious' madness and could include:

- reference to parts of Lear's speech in Act 2 Scene 2 line 290 for your evidence
- consideration of why Lear is particularly mad (furious) at this point in the play
- reference to Lear's tragic decline (peripeteia) and Jacobean ideas of kingship and authority
- analysis of the broken up lines and sentences of this speech and the changes in mood.

....

....

....

....

....

....

....

....

CONTINUED ➡

Questions which invite you to respond to a viewpoint or critical statement

4 These questions will contain a particular interpretation of a specific aspect of the play, such as character, theme or structure. You will need to provide your own take on the given statement.

Examine the view that 'Goneril and Regan are heartless villains and deserve no sympathy at all.'

(a) In the table below, write points which support and points which contest the statement in the question.

POINTS WHICH SUPPORT	POINTS WHICH CONTEST

(b) A student has drafted a paragraph in response to this question. The paragraph has been broken up into sections and included in the table. The student then developed and improved her paragraph. Look at the two versions and write down how the student has change and improved her first attempt.

FIRST ATTEMPT	SECOND ATTEMPT
(A) I completely agree with this view on Goneril and Regan.	(A) Although we can acknowledge Lear's obvious favouritism for Cordelia, this is certainly no justification for their behaviour.
WHAT CHANGES AND IMPROVEMENTS HAS THE STUDENT MADE?	
....	
(B) Regan is massively heartless in the blinding of Gloucester.	(B) For example, Regan sadistically, even gleefully, encourages Cornwall in the blinding of Gloucester.
WHAT CHANGES AND IMPROVEMENTS HAS THE STUDENT MADE?	
....	
(C) 'One side will mock another — th'other too.'	(C) After Cornwall has plucked one of Gloucester's eyes and horrifically stamped on it, Regan demands he plucks 'th'other too.'

CONTINUED ➡

WHAT CHANGES AND IMPROVEMENTS HAS THE STUDENT MADE?

....

....

....

....

(D) This shows how heartless Regan is in King Lear and that she deserves no sympathy at all.	(D) Regan is being dramatically presented here — both through the commanding dialogue and in the stage action — as a tragic villain, who operates in an amoral universe in her desire for power. Furthermore, the unsympathetic presentation of Regan would be seen by feminist critics as confirmation that 'unfeminine' women are shown to be the cause of chaos and cruelty and must be resisted.

WHAT CHANGES AND IMPROVEMENTS HAS THE STUDENT MADE?

....

....

....

....

....

5 **'Edmund is no more than a cruel and ambitious villain.' To what extent do you agree with this view? Remember to include in your answer relevant comment on Shakespeare's dramatic methods.**

Using the improved, 'second attempt' paragraph in the preceding activity as a model, write a paragraph from the middle of an essay in which you **support** the view expressed in this question.

....

....

....

....

....

....

....

....

Now write a paragraph in which you **contest** the view expressed in the question.

....

....

....

CONTINUED ➡

....

....

....

....

....

....

Questions which ask you to analyse an extract and locate its significance to the play as a whole

6   Read the extract from Act 1 Scene 2 of *King Lear*, beginning 'Kent banished thus?' (line 23) and ending 'Abominable villain, where is he?' (line 78). Explore the significance of this extract to the tragedy of the play as a whole. Remember to include in your answer relevant analysis of Shakespeare's dramatic methods.

On a separate piece of paper, write a paragraph in answer to each of these questions. When you have answered all the questions, you will have produced a (very) detailed essay plan.

(a) How does this passage fit within the play as a whole? What have we learnt about Edmund in particular before the passage begins?

(b) How does this passage contribute to the overarching tragedy of *King Lear*? How do Edmund's (and Gloucester's) actions develop the tragedy?

(c) What does this passage reveal about the characters and relationship of Edmund and Gloucester? Remember to quote to support your points.

(d) How does this passage introduce or develop key themes? Again, remember to quote to support your points.

(e) Are there any other distinctive aspects of Shakespeare's dramatic methods or features of tragedy in this passage?

TAKING IT FURTHER

7   Read your answers to the activities in this section of the workbook. Write an essay, under timed conditions, on at least one of the following exam essay questions.

(a) Explore Shakespeare's presentation of disguises in *King Lear*. You must relate your discussion to relevant contextual factors and ideas from your critical reading.

(b) 'The Fool is no more than light comic relief in *King Lear*.' To what extent do you agree with this view? Remember to include in your answer relevant comment on Shakespeare's dramatic methods.

(c) Read the extract from Act 4 Scene 6 of *King Lear*, beginning 'But who comes here?' (line 80) and ending 'Ay, every inch a king' (line 106).

Either,

Explore the significance of this extract to the tragedy of *King Lear*. Remember to analyse Shakespeare's dramatic methods. (AQA style)

Or

With close reference to the language in this extract, explore how Shakespeare presents Lear's state of mind. (Eduqas style)

The publisher would like to thank the following for permission to reproduce copyright material:

Acknowledgments:

p. 6, Bradley, A. C. *Shakespearean Tragedy: Lectures on Hamlet, Othello, King Lear, Macbeth, 2nd ed,* London: Macmillan, 1905; **p. 13, Kastan, D.S.** '"A rarity most beloved": Shakespeare and the Idea of Tragedy' from *A Companion to Shakespeare's Works: The Tragedies*, London: John Wiley & Sons, Inc; **p. 22, Bradley, A.C.** *Shakespearean Tragedy: Lectures on Hamlet, Othello, King Lear, Macbeth, 2nd ed,* London: Macmillan, 1905; **p. 25, McLuskie, K.** 'The Patriarchal Bard: Feminist Criticism and King Lear', Manchester University Press, 2012; **p. 30, Muir, K.** *King Lear (Masterstudies)*, Penguin UK, 1986; **p.30, Kirschbaum, L.** *Character and characterization in Shakespeare*, Wayne State University Press, 1962; **p. 43, Nuttall, A.D.** *Why Does Tragedy Give Pleasure*, Oxford University Press, 1996; **p. 46, Bradley, A.C.** *Shakespearean Tragedy: Lectures on Hamlet, Othello, King Lear, Macbeth,* **2**nd ed, London: Macmillan, 1905; **p. 49, O'Toole, F.** *Shakespeare Is Hard, But So Is Life: A Radical Guide to Shakespearean Tragedy*, Granta UK, 2002; **p. 52,** Lever, J. W. *The Tragedy of State*, Routledge, 1997; **p. 55,** Rutter, C. 'Eel Pie and Ugly Sisters in King Lear' from *Lear from Study to Stage*, Associated University Presses 1997; **p. 58, Swinburne, A.C.** *Poems and Prose*, Read Books Ltd, 2013; **p. 58, Knight, W.** *The Wheel of Fire*, Routledge, 2001; **p. 58, Dollimore, J.** *Radical Tragedy: Religion, Ideology and Power in the Drama of Shakespeare and His Contemporaries*, Circa Publications, 1984; **p. 58, Mack, M.** *King Lear in Our Time*, Routledge, 2001.

Every effort has been made to trace all copyright holders, but if any have been inadvertently overlooked, the Publishers will be pleased to make the necessary arrangements at the first opportunity.

Although every effort has been made to ensure that website addresses are correct at time of going to press, Hodder Education cannot be held responsible for the content of any website mentioned. It is sometimes possible to find a relocated web page by typing in the address of the home page for a website in the URL window of your browser.

Orders: please contact Bookpoint Ltd, 130 Milton Park, Abingdon, Oxon OX14 4SB. Telephone: (44) 01235 827720. Fax: (44) 01235 400454. Lines are open 9.00–17.00, Monday to Saturday, with a 24-hour message answering service. Visit our website at www.hoddereducation.co.uk

ISBN 9781510434936

© Richard Vardy 2018

First published in 2018 by

Hodder Education

An Hachette UK Company,

Carmelite House, 50 Victoria Embankment

London EC4Y 0DZ

Impression number   5 4 3 2 1

Year   2022 2021 2020 2019 2018

Cover photo © nejron/123RF.com

Typeset in Pondicherry, India by Integra Software Services Pvt. Ltd.

Printed in Dubai

A catalogue record for this title is available from the British Library

HODDER EDUCATION

t: 01235 827827

e: education@bookpoint.co.uk

w: hoddereducation.co.uk

ISBN 978-1-5104-3493-6

9 781510 434936